THE ROAD TO CARMEL

Foreword by David Wilkerson

A Couple's Dramatic Journey from Broadway to Mount Carmel

DAVID DAVIS

The Road to Carmel

ISBN 1-56043-336-1

Previously published by **Destiny Image Publishers, Inc.**
as *Valley of Trouble, Mountain of Hope*

Seventh Printing, March 2007
Printed in Israel

*This book is affectionately dedicated
to my wife, Karen, for her love,
devotion, support, and prayers. Her
humility, faith, and perseverance
have been a continual inspiration
to me on our upward climb to God's
"fruitful field" (Carmel).*

Acknowledgments

Thanks to Reuven and Yanit Ross for their insightful comments. Julie Stahl added her very special editing skills. Special thanks to Joy Griffiths, our faithful assistant and devoted friend who went beyond the extra mile typing the manuscript in its various stages of development.

Contents

Quotes from Letters...1

Foreword 3

Prologue 5

1- Broadway..7

2- Israel..23

3- Karen..37

4- Times Square Church 51

5- The Upper Room 71

6- The Call 79

7- Jerusalem...97

8- Mount Carmel...109

9- The Valley of Trouble is the Door of Hope 119

10- War on the Carmel...137

11- House of Victory 147

12- Carmel Assembly 161

13- Drug Wars 175

14- The Spirit & Power of Elijah...................................197

15- Restoring the Altar of the Lord 219

Epilogue 233

Afterword 235

Quotes From Letters

"I couldn't stop reading the book...dramatic and moving."

Margaret, N. Ireland

"[This book] reflects the heart of God for His ancient people Israel...it will be a blessing to many."

Malcolm, S. Africa

"Your wonderful, moving book led me to Times Square Church...and the personal relationship I have finally found with Jesus—accepting Him in my heart as my personal Savior—after years and years of metaphysics and trying a myriad of churches and religions—what was missing was this personal relationship with Jesus...Praise His holy Name forever and ever...."

Luba, New York City

"Thank you for your wonderful book. We are praying for your work."

Singapore

"Your book has challenged me to follow my call."

David, YWAM

"I started reading your book and could not put it down."
John, USA

"What joy and encouragement I received when I read your book. It was so exciting to read how the Lord led you to Mount Carmel."
Mary, England

"It is hard for me to put into words what gripped me about your book. It made me want to weep...to pray with a deeper intensity...and it showed me God's heart."
Jen, S. Africa

"[This book] was a blessing to ourselves and other brothers and sisters in our fellowship."
Ron, England

"I read the book in a day, and apart from our Lord touching my heart with so many tears, I know it will have a long-lasting effect on me...the book brought my prayers to life."
Pauline, England

"[This book] would be a great tool of God's blessing for the church in Slovakia and the Czech Republic. It needs to be printed here."
Stanislav
(translator and publisher of Slovakian edition)

"Bill and I have read [this book] and found it so inspiring that we would like to order further copies to sell through our New Zealand newsletter."
Rachel, New Zealand

Foreword

The Road to Carmel is a miracle story. It is a story that could not be told until these very times in which we live—by this I mean the last days.

Prophecy is rapidly being fulfilled in Israel. House of Victory and Carmel Assembly have been established by the Holy Spirit as part of the fulfillment of God's promise to do a mighty work in Israel before the return of Christ.

Every friend of Israel will thrill at the story of God's leading, His grace, and the operation of the Holy Spirit on the very mountain where Elijah raised an altar to the Lord and slew the false prophets of Baal.

David and Karen Davis are being mightily used of the Lord in pioneering this wonderful last-days witness on Mount Carmel.

Best of all, this book provides living proof that God has not forgotten His covenant with Israel.

David Wilkerson
(Founding Pastor, Times Square Church)

Prologue

Scuds

The air raid siren screamed in the night. I sat up in bed. Missiles! I yelled to Karen, "Get up! Grab your gas mask and run to the bomb shelter." We jumped out of bed in our sweat suits, slipped on our sneakers, and ran for the back door. As Karen went out into the night, I stopped to lock the door. Israeli authorities had told the public that we would have four minutes after a siren sounded before a Scud would hit Haifa. As I fumbled with the key, there was a tremendous explosion. Mount Carmel shook beneath my feet. I almost fell down. Haifa Bay lit up like noonday. I was terrified. "Run!" I screamed. We ran down the steps toward the shelter. There was another deafening roar. The mountain shook again and lit up like daylight. Finally, we stumbled into the bomb shelter.

There was chaos, noise. A baby was screaming as his father tried to put him into his little, plastic tent. An old Arab couple huddled there with their police dog "Rocky." After struggling to don our gas masks, we sat peering at each other, looking like some strange tribe of animals in a cave. I prayed like I'd never prayed. Wanting to hear from God, I got out my Bible and read Hebrews 12:26: "…Yet once more I will shake not only the earth, but also the heaven." God was shaking Israel and His body, and He was certainly shaking me to the core of my being. As I prayed, I sensed in my spirit that He was warning Israel, perhaps one last time, to turn to Him. I realized that I had experienced the wrath and kindness of God in an instant.

We sat in the shelter all night not knowing if we had been attacked by gas or not. Early in the morning, we heard on the radio that the Iraqi ruler, Saddam Hussein, had not sent deadly nerve gas in his missiles.

About 8:00 a.m., we all ventured out of the shelter. The birds were singing! They were alive! Karen and I looked down toward the port of Haifa. It was still there! As we stood gazing, the most beautiful rainbow I have ever seen appeared over Haifa Bay. I began to weep. We clapped our hands. Then we fell to our knees and thanked God. Later, we learned that the first Scud to hit Haifa missed a major oil storage area at the port by about one hundred meters. God's mercies are new every morning.

– Chapter 1 –

Broadway

I stood on stage taking my bows at the curtain call in a Broadway Theatre. The audience applauded and applauded. Then they began to stand. "Bravo! Bravo!" they shouted. It was an actor's dream-come-true. At the last moment Richard Gere, the movie star in the leading role, called in sick. I had replaced the star of a Broadway play on a Friday night with standing room only, having never rehearsed the second act. So much money was at stake that the producers had begged me to perform. Word travels fast in Broadway theatre circles. An understudy saved the show without even rehearsing half of it! Autograph hounds waited at the stage door. I made my way to Sardi's, the theatre restaurant. People pointed and whispered, "That's him."

Later that night in my Greenwich Village apartment I tried to sleep, but I could not. I couldn't come down. In the darkness of my bedroom a thought floated into my head that I couldn't shake, "It doesn't mean anything." I was miserable, lonely, empty. I started crying and couldn't stop. After all the years of struggle and study and training, what did it all mean? At that moment the evening's glory seemed so fleeting, so meaningless. The world I had built didn't make sense anymore. I realized that I was lost and cried myself to sleep.

In high school, I played football and always wanted to play on a college team, but I was too small. At the beginning of my senior year, I broke my ankle and missed the entire season. But that didn't stop me. After high school, I joined the Marine Corps, where I lifted weights and again played football. Three years later, I attended Wake Forest University in North Carolina in order to play football. There, I broke my other ankle, and I realized my football days were finished. Instead, I started acting in plays and fell in love with the theatre. I had finally found my thing. After undergraduate school, I received an M.A. in Theatre from the University of Maryland.

In the late sixties, I moved to Detroit to continue my training and education. I acted for two seasons in a classical, repertory company there and received my Ph.D. in Theatre from Wayne State University in downtown Detroit. It was a turbulent time in Detroit. In 1968, race riots set the downtown area aflame. The National Guard was called in to calm the situation. The university was closed, and we had to flee to Canada to escape the city.

The racial trouble stirred up many questions in my soul and spurred me on to accomplish my theatre goals. I wrote a doctoral dissertation on Hamlet. Shakespeare had become the chief god in my private pantheon, which also included Euripides, Anton Chekhov, and Eugene O'Neill. Then, after two seasons of regional theatre and two college teaching jobs, I moved to New York, where I accepted a position at Fordham University at Lincoln Center for the Performing Arts.

My dream was to combine academic and professional theatre. It seemed to me to be the best of both worlds. I could teach my classes while at the same time acting on a soap opera, Broadway, or off-Broadway. At Fordham, I was elected the Chairman of the Performing Arts Division, which gave me the freedom to create my own classes. My goal was to be on the cutting edge of social issues by working with artists to make a statement that would impact and change society.

Racial issues challenged my soul. I acted in Charles Fuller's "A Soldier's Play," a powerful indictment against racism in America and the second play by a black playwright to win the Pulitzer Prize. I worked with the Negro Ensemble Co. on a number of other plays and won several awards for directing.

For years I had been striving to gain a deeper understanding of the human plight. I believed Shakespeare had the most profound insights. I taught Shakespeare, directed Shakespeare, acted in Shakespeare, and I had even been privileged to play Hamlet, the "role of roles" for an actor. The character of Hamlet has everything—passion, poetry, a full range of emotions. His is the ultimate search for significance…but he doesn't find any answers. His last words are, "The rest is silence."

There is a terrible emptiness that often besets actors when a show closes. It happened to me with Hamlet. The day after the production closed, I returned to the theatre. No one was there. The scenery was gone. Waves of emptiness washed over me. It was finished. It had all been make-believe, and now it remained only as a memory. For me the fantasy-high of acting in the live theatre was always followed by the devastating low of reality. It was one of the reasons that I drank so much alcohol.

Many times, I would come down after a show with a few drinks. I never drank before a show because I was "professional" and had my standards. In my teaching and acting I carried the banners of "excellence" and "purity of art." Theatre was the highest art form, I thought, because it combined all the others.

However, one night while I was on stage with another actor, the truth hit home. We had been in the play together for months. I said my line, but he was looking at me very strangely. Suddenly, I realized I had said *his* line, not mine. I had done the unthinkable and had had a few beers to drink before the show. Although I'd been drinking and getting drunk since I was fifteen, I had denied the truth about myself. Now the truth was inescapable—I was an alcoholic.

Outwardly, it still seemed like I had everything. I went to the Tony Awards at the beautiful Mark Hellinger Theatre in a limousine, drinking champagne and wearing a tuxedo. Nevertheless, success and alcohol did not satisfy me, so I searched for meaning and peace through relationships. Each time I had a new girlfriend, I thought, *This is the one*. But after a time I would hurt her or she would hurt me, and the soured relationship would end in despair. New York can be the loneliest city in the world. Sometimes I would curl up in a fetal position in bed and try not to think about my loneliness.

Once, I played the role of a psychiatrist in the play, "Equus." He was also a man searching for meaning in life.

His final line is, "I have this sharp chain in my mouth, and it never comes out." He was bound because he could not find the truth. I understood.

Finally, shattered by the realization that in spite of all my endeavors my life still had no meaning, I consciously began to search for God. I visited a lovely little historic church in Greenwich Village several times, and after a few weeks, I made an appointment to meet with the pastor. I told him I felt I should become a minister and asked him about attending Bible school. In response, this nice-looking, gentle man asked me if I was a homosexual. He admitted that he was, and so were many of the people attending his church. When I replied that I was not a homosexual, he advised me to stay in my profession, because it was already a "ministry."

Dissatisfied with his response, my search continued. I began to attend another historic Greenwich Village Church in Washington Square. This church had a reputation for being involved in the arts, especially the avant-garde theatre. The pastor did not preach from the Bible, but rather took his sermon material from T.S. Eliot, W.H. Auden, and other poets. Going to church was like going to a lecture. A woman minister, who joined the leadership there, made it clear that she was a lesbian. For her, God's gender was female.

Once a month we had "agape love feasts" at the end of the service. We all brought wine and food, and had a meal together. I liked it, and often got intoxicated. One Sunday morning as we began our "agape feast," the minister uncharacteristically quoted from the Bible, First Corinthians 11:23-24 (NKJ): "...the Lord Jesus on the same night in which He was betrayed took bread; and when He had given thanks, He broke it and said, 'Take, eat; this is My body which is broken for you; do this in remembrance of

Me.'" The Word of God gripped my heart and broke something inside of me. Tears began to roll down my face.

One Sunday morning after a service, an actor friend of mine, who also attended the church, asked if he could talk to me. We crossed the street and sat on a park bench in Washington Square. He explained that he wanted to create an original theatre piece, based on the story of Pentecost, by collaborating with other performers, actors, singers, musicians, and dancers.

"What happened at Pentecost?" I asked.

"The Holy Spirit came," he answered. "I want to dramatize it—put it on a stage—explore it. Let's try to define it, make it relevant."

I was very interested. Throughout the years I had been involved in creating several original theatre events. He suggested that I read the account of what happened at Pentecost and told me that I'd find it in The Acts of the Apostles, Chapter Two.

That afternoon I returned to my apartment and looked for a Bible. There, on one of my bookshelves, tucked among my collections of Shakespeare, the Greeks, the great philosophers, and my "Great Ideas" series, was an old black Bible. I took it down and dusted it. Written on the inside cover was my dormitory address from Wake Forest University. As a college freshman, more than twenty years earlier, I had been obliged to take an Old Testament and New Testament course. I had not opened the book since then. I sat down and looked in the table of contents to find The Acts of the Apostles. I then read Chapter Two.

What struck me first was the radical change in the apostle Peter. I knew that he had been a braggart and then had denied Jesus. But now, this man who had been a coward made an extraordinary speech in public about Jesus,

His crucifixion and resurrection. Not only that, but three thousand people believed what he said. Peter explained that God's Holy Spirit had been poured out on him and the other disciples in fulfillment of the words of the Jewish prophet Joel. He said this power was available to "all who are far off" (Acts 2:39). The actor in me was stirred. I wanted to play Peter, this man who had become new. I phoned my actor/director friend and said, "If I can play Peter, count me in."

We had some strange rehearsals. A black gospel singer joined our peculiar group. She and my actor friend argued constantly. He insisted that we get in touch with "the universal spirit." She insisted that we pray to Jesus. It was the New Age clashing with that "old-time religion." I just listened. Meanwhile I was trying to "get inside" this tough, proud, Jewish fisherman named Peter. How did he walk and talk? As I worked on his Pentecost speech, I began to think, *If this is true, and if this power of the Holy Spirit is still available, this is what I need.* Peter had been transformed by it. Perhaps I could be, too. The production fell apart. No one could agree on what the "spirit" was, or how to dramatize it. But I was hooked on this changed man Peter.

As the months passed, I began to talk to some of my "born-again" theatre students about Pentecost, the Bible, and Jesus. One of them told me that I needed to find a Spirit-filled congregation, but I had no idea what she meant. One day another student was sitting in the lobby of my office. He didn't have an appointment, and I was too busy to talk to him. He waited all afternoon. Finally at about 5:00 p.m., I met with him.

"What can I do for you?" I asked him.

"I know where you can find what you're looking for," he replied.

"I hardly know you," I answered. "How do you know what I need?"

"I have some friends in show business who attend meetings where the Holy Spirit is being poured out."

"Where?" I asked, suddenly interested.

He told me that they met in a music recording studio in Times Square on Wednesdays. Wednesday is matinee day on Broadway. These believing actors, singers, and dancers could perform their shows at 2:00 p.m., have their meeting between shows at 5:30 p.m., and get back to the theatre in time for the evening performance.

It was Wednesday. I looked at my watch. It was 5:15. I looked at my student.

"Let's go," I said.

We walked out of Lincoln Center to the corner of 9th Avenue and 60th Street and jumped into a taxi.

"Ninth and 41st," my young friend told the cab driver.

It was rush hour. Cars were bumper to bumper, barely crawling to the Lincoln Tunnel. We could hardly move. After ten minutes we were only at 58th Street. I gave the driver a dollar and got out of the cab. As I stood on the corner, I thought about the work I had to do and started to return to my office, but something stopped me. I hesitated.

"Let's walk," I said.

It was getting dark as we quickly walked down 9th Avenue. Fifteen minutes later we approached 41st Street. People live in cardboard boxes there. Drug addicts and prostitutes work the block. As we left the street and walked up a set of stairs to the second floor studio, I could hear singing. When we entered the room I saw about 150 people—blacks and whites—all singing. But it wasn't just singing. They were praising and worshiping God and a presence filled the room. I recognized several faces of actors. Someone ushered me to a chair on the center aisle, but I couldn't stand up. I fell to my knees.

Then it happened. I met Jesus. He was brilliant light, all light. I felt so dirty in His presence. I had broken all Ten Commandments and felt crushed by a heavy, intolerable guilt. I wanted to crawl away from Him. Over and over again, I said, "I'm sorry, I'm sorry." To my amazement, the weight on me suddenly lifted. I knew then that I was forgiven. I knew that He had accepted me just the way I was. I couldn't stop crying. The student who brought me was staring at me, and everyone else was singing.

When the singing ended I managed to drag myself into a chair. A young black man began to speak. Everything he said seemed specifically for me, and his words penetrated my heart. How could he know about me? I began to realize that the Holy Spirit was speaking through him. Like Peter, he, too, was new. He was radically changed. It was true! What had happened to Peter had happened to this man, this Broadway performer who stood speaking to me.

After the meeting, I was introduced to several people, including the speaker. As I shook his hand I stared at him, looking for the Spirit that was on him or in him. I glanced around the room and realized I'd come home. Here in a Broadway music studio I'd found Jesus.

Everything changed. I no longer hurried through the streets of New York to audition for films, plays, television shows, or commercials. Instead, I hurried to a music studio in an upper room for Bible studies and meetings. My upbringing and background had left me totally unprepared for the transformation that had taken place. Years of education and my search for knowledge had not filled the void in my heart. Now, I experienced a river of peace deep within me that was beyond my understanding. I was like a man who finds an oasis in the desert. My thirst for this "living water" was insatiable. I couldn't get enough of Jesus. I knew I had found the truth—or rather met the Truth. He had found me. Jesus was alive—radiantly, eternally alive.

I read the Gospels. For years, I had trained myself and others in theatre to mentally and physically put ourselves into the scene on which we were working. We tried to inhabit the characters and the given circumstances, and called it the "magic If." "If" I were this character in these circumstances, what would I do? Now as I read the Gospel of Matthew I felt as if I was right there walking on the shore of the Sea of Galilee with Jesus. As He looked at Peter and John while they fished, I heard Him say, "Follow Me, and I will make you fishers of men." I seemed to move through the scenes with Him. He wasn't just an historical figure from the past anymore; He was present and speaking to me. His words were alive and pierced my soul.

The parable of "The Prodigal Son" moved me deeply. In it, Jesus told the story of a rebellious young man who realizes the error of his ways. After squandering his life and inheritance the young man decides to return to his father and ask for forgiveness. But before he arrives, his father sees him coming, runs a long way to meet him, and greets him with embraces and kisses. Luke 15:24 (NKJ) records that the loving, heart-broken father cried out with joy, "This my son was dead and is alive again; he was lost and is found." It was hard for me to believe that the father actually accepted this son and ran out to meet the one who had so disappointed him. I couldn't imagine a Middle Eastern father, dressed in robes, running to meet his boy like that. I looked at three different translations to make sure that Jesus had told the story that way. It was true. Then I realized how much I had wounded Jesus with my years of selfishness and sin. Others had stopped loving me, and I had stopped loving them—but not Jesus. He had never stopped loving me, waiting for me, and longing for me to come home. Such love was difficult for me to grasp. Over the desk in my office at the university I hung a card that read:

"This My son was dead and is alive again; He was lost and is found."

My character and my lifestyle began to change. Prior to coming to know Jesus, I only cared about myself. In fact, for years I had even taught that self-fulfillment was the highest goal in life. Humanism was my religion, and I was my own god. Now I began to care about the lost people walking the streets of New York. For the first time, I saw their faces—drug addicts, alcoholics, people talking to themselves. Poor and homeless people lived in cardboard boxes, while others in fur coats and tuxedos stepped around them to get into limousines. I wanted to help the poor people, to give them what I had, but I didn't know how. My speech also began to change. I was embarrassed to hear the filth that came out of my mouth, and I knew that it was offensive to the Lord.

One day at a meeting in the music studio, a visiting evangelist/singer preached a message and then invited the congregants to come forward for prayer. When the man laid his hands on me, something happened. I couldn't stand up. I fell on my knees and wept uncontrollably. One of the leaders gave me a paper towel. Then he gave me some more. Finally he gave me the whole roll. I tried to get up, but couldn't. I felt so utterly unworthy. All I could do was thank Jesus over and over again. I don't know how long I did this. Time seemed to stop. I was in His glorious presence and that was all that mattered. As my gratitude began to turn to joy, I started to praise Jesus in a new language. It was like a love language, enabling me to converse more intimately with Him. I felt such joy that I didn't care that I was a Ph.D., kneeling on the floor of a music studio in Times Square, clutching a roll of paper towels, and talking in an unknown language. Later, I realized that what had happened to Peter and the 120 at that first Pentecost, had happened to me. I had been filled with the Holy Spirit according to His Word. It was true—this gift was available today.

It bothered me that I still drank, even though Alcoholics Anonymous had taught me that I would be an alcoholic for life, even if I stopped drinking. One night shortly after my "Broadway Pentecost," I was watching a football game on television with friends and drinking beer. I was very uncomfortable and didn't enjoy myself. That night before I went to sleep, I told Jesus I wanted to stop drinking and how sorry I was and asked Him to help me. The next morning when I awoke, the desire to drink was gone. From that day, I have never wanted or taken an alcoholic drink. I was totally free and no longer an alcoholic. Jesus had heard my prayer and answered me.

That spring our fellowship joined another congregation on a "praise cruise" in the Bahamas. This multiracial group of "show business-types," held meetings in the nightclub of the ship. What singing! What worship! These Broadway singers could really praise the Lord.

Before leaving New York I had asked if I could be baptized during the cruise. I had studied about baptism and understood that as I went under the water I would be making a public statement that my "old man," my old way of life, was being "buried with Him," and that "just as Christ was raised from the dead by the glory of the Father," I, too, should "walk in newness of life" (Rom. 6:4 NKJ).

Just before dawn on the morning of my baptism, I dreamed that my mother was in heaven and was calling the ship. A friend of mine answered the phone.

"Is David there? It's his mother calling from heaven."

"He's on shore with the others," my friend replied.

Then my mother said, "Tell him I will be at his baptism."

As I woke up the dream seemed more real to me than the compartment in which I was sitting, and I knew my mother was in heaven!

More than ten years earlier my younger brother had called to tell me that my sixty-year-old mother had just had a heart attack. She was in Georgetown Hospital in Washington, D.C. and the doctors expected her to recover. My mother and father had been married at Georgetown University Chapel, where my father had attended graduate school. Now my mother was about to retire from her high school teaching job.

I was acting in a play in Providence, Rhode Island. Since I didn't have the money to fly, I decided to drive to Washington. I explained to the director of the play that I needed to leave immediately, and they prepared the understudy to play my part that night. After driving for eight hours, I arrived at Georgetown Hospital in the late afternoon. I found the floor where my mother was.

"Can you tell me where Mrs. Davis is?" I asked a doctor anxiously.

"Oh, she died," he said.

"When?" I asked.

"A couple of hours ago." He walked away.

I went into a phone booth and sobbed. I wanted to talk to her, to tell her I loved her, and how sorry I was for all the pain I had caused her. But I was too late. My brother told me later that one of the last things she said was, "I'm so glad David is coming."

I was baptized on a lovely summer afternoon on a beach in the Bahamas, with an actor named Abraham, and another brother named Luke, who later died of AIDS. As I came out of the water I felt like football pads were falling off my shoulders and body into the water. As I made my way back to the shore, fifty or more of our group stood on the beach, singing and praising Jesus. Through the palm trees the Caribbean sun was setting behind them so that they were lit from behind and I couldn't see their faces. I fell on my knees on the beach and looked up at them.

I knew I had a new family. These people were my new brothers and sisters. My mother, father, and older brother were all dead and for years I had longed for family. Now, God in His mercy had given me a new one.

Later, laying in a hammock on the island, I began to thank God for my new family. I tried to understand what had happened to me. I knew it was a turning point. As I thought and prayed, the Holy Spirit impressed upon me that I must go to Israel—to the Holy Land where Jesus had lived. I couldn't stop thinking about it, and it quickly turned into an intense desire. When we returned to New York I booked a flight to Israel immediately. Several days later I landed at David Ben Gurion Airport in Tel Aviv.

Chapter 2

Israel

My first destination was Jerusalem. Looking out of the window as we began the ascent to the Holy City, the beauty of the rolling Judean hills arrested me. Winding our way up to Jerusalem, I thought of the ancient and modern wars that had been fought for this highway—Assyrian, Babylonian, Roman, Crusader, Turkish, British, and others. Burned-out tanks and military vehicles strewn on the hillsides by the road served as reminders of Israel's recent battles for this pass during her 1948 War of Independence.

History flowed through my veins. Both of my parents had strong connections to our American heritage. My father, an historian, delighted in telling us stories of American heroes like George Washington and Abraham Lincoln. Our summer vacations were often spent visiting Civil War battlefields like Gettysburg. My mother was a proud descendant of an American Revolutionary War hero and one of the early American presidents, William Henry Harrison.

Later, I tramped through Europe myself, exploring and studying what I called, "the thrill of history." I was especially interested in Greece and the Greek Isles, the birthplace of democracy. In my opinion, democracy was the highest achievement of mankind. I remember standing in the Theatre of Dionysis, the god of theatre, wine, and sex, in Athens and thinking, *It all started here.*

Sitting in the taxi on my way to Jerusalem, I was experiencing something entirely different. In Greece, I had been searching and longing for the truth, for the eternal, but I only found what man had to offer. Now I knew the Truth. The search had ended. My heart's cry was to understand more deeply this eternal truth and to know the true God who had revealed Himself to me.

There was something very moving about my first glimpse of Jerusalem. This city has been at the center of the world's attention for three thousand years. I wanted to explore it and to understand its significance in my life.

King David ruled here. His son, Solomon, built the temple to the one true God here. Jesus was crucified and resurrected here. From here, He ascended into Heaven, and to the Mount of Olives, He will return. Now I was here! I sensed God had drawn me to Israel and Jerusalem to be alone with Him, but I had no idea what plans He had in store for me.

I reserved a room in a five-star hotel for my first night in Israel. I had decided I would simply trust God to show me where to go and to stay after my first night. As I lay on the bed in my hotel room, I read my Bible and thanked God for bringing me to "the Golden City," the "City of Truth." I realized that I was on a spiritual pilgrimage, and that I wasn't here to sightsee and marvel at historical ruins. Those days were gone. I longed to hear the voice of

God, to connect with His Spirit in a deeper way, without any hindrances. However, I still felt dirty before Him.

Since my college days, I had been addicted to sex and pornography. I think it started with *Playboy* Magazine during the sexual revolution of the sixties. I wanted to be free of all of it, especially now. I told Jesus that I was sorry for my years of immorality and that I wanted to be free and clean. I told Him I never wanted to lust after another woman or look at another dirty picture. As I lay on the bed, I put my open Bible on my chest and asked Him to help me. Something lifted. There, in that hotel room in Jerusalem, Jesus set me free from my sexual addiction.

The next morning I checked out of the hotel. On the recommendation of a few local Christians, I took a room at the YMCA for a week. The "Y," a beautiful old Middle Eastern building facing the King David Hotel and the Old City, was within walking distance of everything. I immediately set off for the Old City.

As I wandered through the crowded, narrow streets and alleys for the first time, I asked the Lord to direct my steps. Jews, Arabs, and tourists hustled along the stone corridors, making deals and hawking their wares. Through the buzz of activity, my thoughts turned to the Garden of Gethsemane, and so I headed in that direction. Leaving the Old City through the Damascus Gate, I made my way around the outside of the walled city and down into the Kidron Valley. From there, I began the steep climb onto the lower slope of the Mount of Olives. When I arrived at Gethsemane, facing the Old City, a monk ushered me into the garden, where I found a secluded corner. I was alone.

Sitting under an ancient olive tree, I read the Gospel accounts of Jesus' agony in this very garden. I was struck by His desire for His followers to pray while He prayed.

He knew their need for prayer at that critical hour, but instead, they fell asleep. Jesus, left alone, cried out to His Father. His flesh did not want to go to the cross. This sinless man recoiled at the thought of taking the sin of the world upon Himself. Yet, He laid down His own will and chose crucifixion for me. The decision that had changed the world had happened right here.

Like Peter, I told my Lord, "I wouldn't have run away." But as I honestly thought about that night, I realized I, too, would have run away. The loneliness of Jesus touched me deeply. He understood my loneliness and was filling it with His love for me. I stayed in the garden a long time, and as I returned to the Old City, I knew that I was no longer alone.

Entering the Old City walls, I walked the Via Dolorosa. Traditionally, it is believed that Jesus stumbled down this "way of sorrow" carrying His cross to Golgotha. Once again, I read about the events that surrounded Jesus' crucifixion. They lied about Him, spit on Him, beat Him, stripped Him, and crowned Him with thorns. Finally, they crucified Him. From that lonely cross, He actually asked His Father to forgive them—to forgive me. There, I asked Jesus to help me be like Him.

I started going to meetings of believers in Jerusalem. On Sunday morning after a meeting in Christ Church at Jaffa Gate in the Old City, I was having some refreshments when an older lady with white hair came up and introduced herself to me. I had noticed her in other meetings. She said that she was from the States and was a volunteer nurse in a hospital in Jerusalem. She was going to visit an Arab family in the Old City and asked me if I wanted to come along.

I followed my new friend Betty through the crowded maze of the Old City. We stopped at a locked metal gate built into an ancient stone archway. A small, low metal door that served as an entrance was ajar. We could only enter one at a time. Betty told me that this was referred to as the "eye of the needle." In times past, the diminutive door was used mainly as a means of protection against invaders and thieves. Jesus referred to these kinds of doors in Matthew 19:24 when He said, "And again I say to you, it is easier for a camel to go through the eye of a needle, than for a rich man to enter the kingdom of God."

Betty and I stooped to enter the narrow door, one at a time, which opened into a courtyard. We climbed a flight of ancient stone steps and were greeted by a middle-aged Arab couple and their fifteen-year-old daughter, Sabrina.

Ibrahim and Frida invited us into their sitting room. The low, concave ceiling gave the room the appearance of a cave filled with old oriental furniture, a lot of books, and a television set.

However, no matter how humble the abode, you cannot visit Arab people in their home without partaking of the best of their hospitality. Frida served us a most delicious, savory meal called *maklubi*, which means "upside down" in Arabic. Chicken, cauliflower, and rice are cooked together and seasoned with aromatic spices. Afterward the entire dish is flipped upside down. We feasted and then drank the sweet black Arabic coffee.

In the Middle East, eating together symbolizes that in fact there is a friendly relationship between the diners. Only after you have eaten can you then discuss the matter at hand.

We conversed in English. Ibrahim was originally from Jordan. Both he and his wife had grown up as members of the Greek Orthodox Church in Jerusalem.

Frida told us that she had breast cancer and was afraid of dying. She told us that she knew Jesus and had even been healed by Him in the past. Some years prior to this time, Ibrahim and Sabrina both confirmed, Jesus had appeared to Frida and healed her back in the very room where we were sitting.

Before we said good-bye, Betty prayed for the family. Frida asked me if I would visit her the next day and pray for her to be healed. The request surprised me. I had never prayed for healing for anyone. I hesitated, but then I agreed to return the next day and to pray.

The following morning, I went to David's Tower near Jaffa Gate and climbed up on the Old City walls to pray. Armed with my Walkman and worship tapes, I spent the morning praying and praising the Lord. I prayed in English and in my prayer language, trying to obey Jude 20, by "building [myself] up in my most holy faith; praying in the Holy Spirit." I asked the Lord to heal Frida and reminded Jesus of the people He had healed in Jerusalem. After a time, I felt like I was soaring in the Spirit. A tremendous assurance of faith arose within me, and I believed Jesus was going to heal Frida.

At lunchtime I entered through the "eye of the needle" into the courtyard, ascended the steps, and was welcomed again into the little sitting room. Of course I was expected to eat another wonderful meal with Frida and Ibrahim. After we finished, Frida asked me to pray for her. She said she believed Jesus could heal her.

I put my hands on her shoulders and began to pray in Jesus' name. I didn't pray long. Simply, I asked Him to heal her, to remove the cancerous tumor from her breast. She cried and thanked me, and we said goodbye.

Again I walked down the Via Dolorosa and left the Old City through Damascus Gate. This time, I was on my way to the Garden Tomb. The Garden Tomb contains a first-century tomb that many believe could actually have been the temporary grave of Jesus. Adjacent to it is a rock cliff with several caves cut into the face of it, giving it the appearance of a skull. Golgotha, where Jesus was crucified, means "place of a skull" in Hebrew.

In the midst of busy, dirty eastern Jerusalem, the Garden Tomb is a place of tranquillity. The Garden Tomb and Gethsemane were the two places in Jerusalem where I felt closest to Jesus. I wanted to spend my last afternoon in Jerusalem here with the Lord before I drove north the following morning to Galilee for the final week of my journey.

I sat there and quietly read the Gospel accounts of what had happened at the tomb of Jesus. Mary Magdalene came to the tomb that Sunday morning while it was still dark. The huge stone, sealed and guarded by all those Roman soldiers, had been rolled away. She ran to tell Peter, and he and John ran to the tomb. They entered the tomb and found it empty. The two disciples went home, but Mary stayed and wept. As she wept, a man she thought was the gardener asked her, "Woman, why are you weeping? Whom are you seeking?" Then He simply said her name, "Mary." It was Jesus—He was alive! How precious it was to be in that place. It made no difference whether the memorialized Garden Tomb was the actual tomb or not. Jesus had risen from the dead and was alive. This was no "magic If," no "willing suspension of disbelief." This historical event had changed my life eternally.

The next morning about 7:00 a.m. the phone rang. It was Betty and she was excited.

"David, thank God I caught you before you left for Galilee."

"Why, what is it?"

"Frida has been healed!" she exclaimed excitedly.

"What? How do you know?" I asked, stunned.

"After you left her she went to the hospital. They X-rayed her and the tumor is gone. The doctor said it was a miracle."

"Are you sure?" I checked.

"I spoke to the doctor myself. She's healed!" Betty reiterated. "Oh, by the way, I've made a reservation for you at the Scottish Hospice in Tiberias on the Sea of Galilee," she said. "They have a room for you. You'll love it. I'm late for work, but I'm so glad I caught you! Hallelujah! Good-bye." She hung up.

As I sat there on my bed, I knew He is the same yesterday, today and, yes, forever.

I drove north from Jerusalem through Samaria, commonly known as the West Bank, on my way to Nazareth, Jesus' hometown. The territories were relatively safe in the days before the "intifada," the Arab uprising that began in 1987. Outside Nablus, the biblical city of Shechem, I stopped at Jacob's Well. It was there that a tired, thirsty Jesus met the Samaritan woman. She had come to draw her daily supply of water from the well, but instead, she met a Jewish man who promised to give her "living water," even a "well of water springing up to eternal life" (Jn. 4: 14). As He told this poor, lost lady all about her life, she confessed that she knew the Messiah was coming. Then

Jesus revealed Himself to her. "I who speak to you am He" (Jn. 4:26b). Jews had no dealings with Samaritans, but Jesus did. He broke down racial barriers and went where others would not go.

As I continued my journey north from Jacob's Well, I rolled down the windows to drink in all I could. A young Israeli soldier was hitchhiking. I thought about picking him up, but he was carrying an automatic weapon. I didn't like the way Israeli soldiers seemed so careless about their weapons. In restaurants and on buses I had seen soldiers who did not seem to notice that the muzzles of their guns were sometimes pointing at someone. More than once one was pointed at me. I knew that their weapons weren't loaded, but in the Marines we had been taught never to point a rifle at anyone unless we intended to kill him. In fact, American Marines were severely disciplined for just such an infraction.

As I watched the Israeli soldier recede in my rearview mirror, the Holy Spirit told me to go back and give him a ride. I didn't want him to sit in the front seat of the car with his Uzi on his lap pointing at me. There, driving through Samaria, past where Ahab and Jezebel had built their temple to a false god, I found myself arguing with the True God. I simply refused to go back, and I knew I was disobeying Him.

Half an hour later, I was completely lost. The map didn't make sense anymore. I drove into a Muslim village, got out of the car, and showed the map to a man there. I told him I wanted to go to Nazareth. He looked at me blankly, gestured for me to wait, and slowly walked away. I waited in what seemed to be the village square. After some time, the man sauntered back with an auto mechanic who was cleaning the grease off of his hands. He took my map, looked at it, and shook his head.

"Nazareth," I said emphatically. "Nazareth…Jesus… Nazareth, where Jesus lived," I repeated slowly.

He just stared at me. A crowd of shopkeepers and others began to gather. I was aggravated at myself for not having picked up that soldier.

"Lord, help me get out of here," I prayed silently. There I stood in the middle of an Arab village somewhere in Samaria. I guess everyone was coming to see the novelty of a lost American. Someone brought Arabic coffee. We all drank coffee and smiled at each other.

After our coffee break, a man who had been studying the map said, "Oh! *Natzeret!*" "Right! Right!" I said relieved. "*Natzeret!*"

He pointed to Nazareth and showed me a back road I needed to take to get there. Somehow I had detoured several miles off the main road. I thanked them and we all shook hands. I waved good-bye as I drove away on the dusty, narrow back road. I promised the Lord that from then on I would pick up every Israeli soldier I saw hitchhiking. I did. I was also faithful to tell each one about his Messiah.

Late in the afternoon my car climbed up to Nazareth. It was a dark and depressing town, and it seemed like it was under a curse. I remembered that Jesus did not do many miracles there because of their unbelief. In fact, some persons in His synagogue had tried to cast Him off a cliff, because He had preached about Elijah and Elisha ministering to people from Lebanon and Syria. It is sad to know that, "…passing through their midst, He went His way" (Lk. 4:30). His own hometown had missed the One for whom they had waited.

As a young man, Jesus had moved from Nazereth to the Sea of Galilee where His public ministry began. That was where I headed next. The sun was beginning to set as I rounded a bend in the road and saw the silver-blue, shimmering sea surrounded by the golden hills of Galilee. My spirit lifted with anticipation.

I stayed at the Scottish Hospice as Betty had arranged for me. The buildings, which overlook the sea, were about one hundred years old. Originally the compound had been used as a hospital, run by Christians from Scotland. The doctor who had founded the hospital, planted eucalyptus trees on the swampy grounds that had helped to heal the land. He had worked among Arabs and Jews and had led a much-persecuted rabbi to the Lord. The Scottish doctor and his wife were buried just below my room.

For several, glorious days I explored the Galilee. One afternoon I sat alone on the sloping hillside of the Mount of Beatitudes overlooking the Sea, and read the Sermon on the Mount where Jesus had spoken it. I longed to live that way—loving my enemies, going the extra mile, not serving two masters any more, only Him. I told Him I wanted to seek His kingdom first, and that I hungered and thirsted after righteousness. I wanted to be pure in heart so I could see more of Him. He replied with words from Matthew 7:13: "Enter by the narrow gate; for the gate is wide, and the way is broad that leads to destruction." I thanked Him for coming to get me on Broadway, and I asked Him to help me walk the narrow way.

On the northern end of the Sea of Galilee are the ruins of Capernaum. Peter, and later Jesus Himself, lived in this fishing village. I spent one day there reading and pondering about the miracles that Jesus performed in and around the ancient synagogue whose foundations are still visible. He healed the lepers and the paralyzed. He cast out demons with a word and healed every kind of disease and sickness (see Mt. 9:35).

As I sat there on an ancient stone, an Israeli tour guide and two German tourist couples got out of a car. The guide read from the Bible about how Jesus had raised the synagogue official's daughter from the dead, and he even pointed out the remains of the synagogue. I was amazed. A Jew reading the New Testament to Germans! Then he closed his Bible and said, "I'm Jewish, so of course I don't believe this." A wave of grief and sadness washed over me. I wondered how he could be so close and yet so far from the truth and how the Lord would reach His own people.

One morning I sat on the shore at daybreak at the spot where the resurrected Jesus appeared to Peter and the others after they returned to fishing. Jesus stood on the beach at dawn and called out to the disciples in the boat: "Cast the net on the right-hand side of the boat, and you will find a catch" (Jn. 21:6). I laughed as I imagined them trying to haul in their catch. When they realized it was the Lord, Peter threw himself into the sea and swam to the shore to meet Jesus. What a breakfast they had on that beach, eating fish with Jesus! As I laughed aloud, I realized someone was standing behind me. I turned and saw an old Franciscan monk staring at me.

"Isn't Jesus wonderful?" I said joyfully. I don't know if he understood English—he just turned and walked away.

It was here that Jesus asked Peter if he loved Him. "Feed My sheep," He told him.

As I sat there and read His next words to Peter, I realized that Jesus was also speaking to me: "Truly, truly, I say to you, when you were younger, you used to gird yourself, and walk wherever you wished; but when you grow old, you will stretch out your hands, and someone else will gird you, and bring you where you do not wish to go" (Jn. 21:18).

My time in Israel was drawing to a close. Early the next morning I would return to America, a changed man. I drove west across Galilee toward the Mediterranean and the port city of Haifa. I wanted to pray on Mount Carmel.

True to my promise to the Lord, I picked up a nice young Israeli soldier who graciously showed me the road to Mount Carmel. He didn't point his rifle at me. I explained to him that Jesus was a Jew and that the Scriptures proved that He was the Jewish Messiah. I told him that many people who called themselves "Christians" were not really followers of Yeshua (Jesus in Hebrew). They had done terrible things to the Jews in His name and I was sorry. I encouraged him to investigate Yeshua for himself and he agreed.

On the northern tip of Mount Carmel at a place called Stella Maris, I sat and looked out over the Mediterranean Sea and thanked God for bringing me to Israel. I felt so close to Him. I didn't understand all that had happened, but I knew it was significant. Something was happening to my heart. I had begun to feel at home in Israel.

As I started to drive away, I decided to turn on the radio for the first time in two weeks to try to find news in English. As I turned the dial on the radio, all of a sudden I heard a song in English.

The rich baritone voice sang, "It is finished," Jesus' last words on the cross. The music filled the car as the voice and choir sang over and over, "It is finished...It is finished..." I stopped on the side of the road on Mount Carmel. I recognized the voice! It was Archie Dennis, the man who had laid hands on me when I was baptized in the Holy Spirit. I began to sob uncontrollably. God was speaking to me on Mount Carmel through a man I knew on the radio. The song ended, and the station seemed to fade.

Was it from Lebanon, thirty miles to the north? I didn't care. It didn't matter. The presence of God was in the car. Tears poured out as if a floodgate had been opened deep inside me. Slowly I drove down Mount Carmel to the sea and pondered what it all meant.

– Chapter 3 –

Karen

When the fall semester began at the university, I was very excited about the Lord. I hired Ben Harney, a close friend and elder at my fellowship, to teach acting. Harney, an award-winning actor and singer, was also an extraordinary teacher who poured himself into the students. Together we prayed for revival among the students.

My new life impacted everything in which I was involved. I began to share the gospel with my colleagues. I tried to combine the gospel with Shakespeare, who often quoted the Bible in his plays. I directed a "born-again" version of King Lear. We held a gospel concert at the university, and several students came to the Lord. My friends also noticed the radical change in me, and I took every opportunity to share the gospel with them.

One afternoon I sat with my best friend Charley in a tavern in Soho. He was a very talented painter, and we had collaborated on several theatre productions. He had been an alcoholic for years. He drank beer and smoked

Marlboros, while I sipped a coke. I told him how I had met Jesus and that I was now free from alcohol and cigarettes.

"Don't tell me you believe in that old-fashioned sin stuff?" he retorted. Later, he ran out of the bar into the middle of West Broadway, screaming, "Get away from me! Get away from me!"

Every day I studied the Bible and also attended a Bible school in the Bronx. The Word of God was full of adventure and revelation to me. I never missed a meeting in the recording studio. Sometimes we had all-night prayer meetings. I found prayer to be hard work, so I just read the Bible in the prayer meetings.

When winter arrived, I began to spend time with a sixty-five-year-old black woman in our congregation. Erma Lee Jackson, or "Mother Jackson" as we called her, was our oldest member. She was a spiritual mother to many of the "new babes." In fact she had stood on the beach with us in the Bahamas when I was baptized. I knew that day that God had given me a new mother.

I often met Mother for lunch. She talked. I listened. As a child, growing up in Richmond, Virginia, her mother had taught her the Word of God. Mother recounted wonderful stories of God's love and the power of prevailing prayer. During the Great Depression, which started in 1929, her family often had no food. Her mother would set the table, call the children to sit down, and pray. Eventually someone would knock on the door with a turkey, a chicken, or a bag of potatoes. God never failed them.

For years, Mother Jackson's alcoholic brother lived on the streets of New York. She never stopped interceding for him. One day, he came to her apartment in Harlem. She gave him a bath, prayed with him, and he accepted the Lord. Soon after, he was set free from alcohol.

Mother had also been healed from breast cancer. A large tumor the size of a golf ball disappeared after she asked the Lord to heal her. I told her about Frida in Jerusalem and that I had received a letter from Betty that confirmed Frida's healing.

"Of course. Jesus heals," Mother shrugged.

At the mid-week meeting a week before my birthday, on February 5, I asked the Lord to show me how to celebrate the day. As I opened my eyes they rested on Mother Jackson. I thought, *I know, I'll take Mother out to dinner. She'll love that.*

After the service I asked her, "Would you like to have dinner with me next week on my birthday?"

"Oh, I would be honored," she said. Standing next to Mother was her thirty-five-year-old roommate whom I hardly knew. Karen, a Jewish believer, worked in the fashion industry and also sang with the worship team in the congregation. She and Mother were a very odd couple. This slender, young shoe model and singer, paired with sixty-five-year-old Erma Lee Jackson, who ran around New York in her white Reeboks, called each other "mother" and "daughter." They seemed to be inseparable.

"Karen, would you like to join us for my birthday dinner?" I asked to be polite. "Yes. Thank you," she accepted graciously.

On my birthday, I took the subway from Greenwich Village up to West 72nd Street, where Mother and Karen shared a small, two-room studio apartment. I buzzed the intercom, and they came down. We walked several, chilly blocks up Columbus Avenue to the Museum Cafe across from the Museum of Natural History. Karen gave me a copy of Andrew Murray's book, *Like Christ*. The book was lying on the table as the waitress came to take our order. When she commented on it, all three of us started to tell her about Jesus.

As we ate, I noticed that Mother Jackson was unusually quiet. She often remarked about her own "gift of gab." Karen began to talk about deep things she had been seeing in the Bible. As she spoke, I realized that this woman was in love with Jesus. She didn't seem interested in me as a man. She was interested in Him. It was refreshing and also disarming. There were no flirtatious, man-woman games going on at the table. She seemed to have such integrity, such intelligence and depth.

As I looked across the table at this beautiful woman I had hardly noticed before this evening, the strangest thing happened to me. I heard in my spirit, "This is your wife." I just stared at her. Then I looked at Mother, who just smiled and sipped her coffee. We left the restaurant, and I walked between Karen and Mother. We stopped at their door.

"Karen, could I see you again?"

"Yes. That would be nice," she smiled and said simply.

We made a date for another night. I said goodnight and walked toward the subway station in a daze. I had met the woman whom God was preparing for me.

Later that week, as we sat in the candlelight of a quiet restaurant, I listened as Karen told me her remarkable story:

> "I grew up in Detroit in an upper, middle class Jewish family. Although we went to synagogue on all the Jewish holidays, the real religion

in our home was humanism. Intellectual achievement and education seemed to be celebrated above all else. I don't think any of us, except maybe my mother, really believed in the God of Abraham, Isaac, and Jacob. My father is an automotive engineer. My mother died of cancer when I was in college. One of my two brothers died of a drug overdose when he was nineteen years old. My other brother is a jazz musician and psychiatrist here in New York.

"Growing up, I trained in classical music and later studied painting at an art school in Philadelphia. Then I moved here to New York to be part of the art scene. I continued to develop my musical ability through vocal training and song-writing workshops, and I've earned a living by working as a shoe model for the high-fashion company, Charles Jourdan.

"For years, I searched for eternal truth. I believed God was the creative spirit behind the beauty and harmony of music and art that so stirred my soul. I longed to tap into this force, and so I plunged deeply into various New Age and occult practices. After many years of trying one technique after another, I still felt an empty place in my heart. I tried to fill that emptiness through romantic relationships with men, but instead, I suffered many disappointments.

"Finally one day, I realized that I was tired and worn out, and I had no answers left to make my life work. I knocked on the door of a friend who lived in my building, thinking that maybe she would have some advice for me. Camille

opened the door. 'Do you have a few minutes?'
I asked her. 'I need someone to talk to.'

"Camille and I had been friends for two years.
She seemed to have her life together. She was
an actress and comedienne who worked on
the children's TV series, 'Sesame Street,' and
created new characters for the 'Muppet' mov-
ies. She had a peace about her that was different from my other friends who meditated,
chanted, and talked a lot about 'inner peace.'
Sometimes I saw her carrying a Bible and
wondered how someone so sophisticated and
intelligent as Camille would be interested in
such an old-fashioned book.

"Occasionally Camille gave me tickets to a
gospel concert and I went. I was always deeply
moved by the music and wept all through
the singing. *These people have the spirit!* I
thought. But then there would be an invita-
tion to receive Jesus and I would run out, saying to myself, *I'm Jewish. This doesn't have
anything to do with me.*

"As I sat in Camille's apartment that day, I
poured my heart out to my friend, who just
listened. When I finished, I asked if she had
any advice for me.

" 'Would you like to pray?' she asked.

" 'I've never done that before.' I thought for a
moment, then answered. 'Why not? I've tried
everything else. I'll try it.'

"Camille led me in a brief prayer in which
I repeated the words after her. I asked God
to help me and I admitted I could not save

myself. I also asked Jesus to forgive my sins, even though I didn't really know what sin was. Then I asked Jesus to come into my heart. I thought to myself that maybe He was another 'master.' When I finished the prayer, I turned to her. 'But, Camille, this couldn't be the only way!' I chided her.

"She simply looked at me and said, 'It is.'

"At that moment the Spirit of Truth pierced my heart like a knife, cutting through all my preconceived ideas and the cherished philosophies by which I had lived. Although I couldn't explain it, I knew I had heard the truth. Truly 'flesh and blood' had not revealed it to me.

"Suddenly I remembered a dream I had had the previous night. In the dream I was in a room with a bright light, but after some time the light grew dim. Then I saw another room with a bright light and went into it. After a while, the same thing happened. I went from room to room always with the same result. Finally, I came out onto an open field with brilliant sunlight. Then the scene switched to the poorest section of downtown New York City, where a group of children were on their knees begging for bread. The next thing I saw was a curtain ripped from top to bottom, and I woke up.

"That morning the dream didn't make sense to me, so I forgot it. Now I understand that it was a picture of my life, of my long search for 'the true light' that gives light to every man (see Jn. 1:9).

"Because I had never read the New Testament, I didn't know that Jesus said, 'I am the Light of the world' (Jn. 8:12), or 'I am the living Bread that comes down from heaven' (Jn. 6:51), or that unless you come to Him as a little child, you cannot enter the kingdom of God (Mt. 18:3). I didn't know that the veil in the temple in Jerusalem had been torn from top to bottom when Jesus died on the cross during Passover. I didn't even know that no one could go beyond the veil into the Holy of Holies except the high priest on Yom Kippur, the Day of Atonement.

"Now I understood that in His great love and mercy God had allowed me to suffer many severe disappointments in order to bring me to the end of myself, to humble me, and to cause me to turn to Him. Through the atoning blood of the Lamb of God, Jesus, the veil over my Jewish heart was removed. Jeremiah 29:13 says, 'And you will seek Me and find Me, when you search for Me with all your heart.'

"Before I left that day, Camille gave me a New Testament, and assured me that as I read it, God would begin to answer my many questions and confirm to me who this Jesus was. I re-turned to my apartment and began to read the Gospel of Matthew. I noticed that it was all so Jewish. Jesus was a Jew, and so were His first fol-lowers. I devoured the Bible. In the following weeks I saw how the Old Testament and the New Testament were one book. The New fulfilled the promises of the Old.

"For the first time in my life, I began to realize what it meant to be Jewish, that God had called out a people for Himself to know Him personally, to share Him with the rest of humanity, and to be a 'light to the Gentiles.'

"As I continued to call upon the Messiah of Israel, Jesus, the love of God began to stream into my heart. Old hurts faded away as a new joy and peace took over. No longer can I sing romantic songs of human love, promoting a message of false hope to the world. Now my desire is to sing of the true love of my life, of the One whose love has touched and healed the deepest places in my soul...."

As I looked at Karen through the candlelight, I was deeply moved by her story. I was falling in love. It was all so different, so pure, so clean, so right.

Five weeks later, I decided to propose to Karen. I discussed my plans with Mother Jackson. At first, I thought it would be romantic to propose in a horse-drawn carriage in Central Park, but Mother and I came up with a better plan. Karen had invited me to dinner at their apartment to cook for me for the first time. I told her that after the meal I had an important question to ask her. Dressed in my tuxedo and laden with gifts, I took a cab from Greenwich Village to West 72nd Street. In two big shopping bags I carried a dozen red roses, a covenant I had written on a large scroll, an antique glass oil lamp, and a new leather Bible on which was engraved the new name, "Karen Janeway Davis."

I rang their lobby intercom and announced: "It's Boaz, for Ruth."

Mother answered: "This is Naomi. Come on up, Boaz."

She buzzed me in. I took the elevator up to their 7th floor apartment and rang the bell. Mother opened the door and tried to act surprised. Karen was cooking at the stove, barefoot and wearing an apron. She turned around and we looked at each other.

"What's all this?" she asked quite surprised.

"I told you I had something important to ask you after dinner. But I'd like to ask you right now." I took her by the hand.

"What? What? Wait! Let me take off my apron," she protested, embarrassed by my sudden action.

I knelt down on one knee in the middle of the kitchen, took out the scroll, unrolled it slowly, and read:

> "COVENANT: Be it known to all the world that KAREN JANEWAY (the bride) is consecrated and set apart for DAVID DAVIS (the bridegroom) as he promises to pay the "Bride price" of his UNENDING LOVE, DEVOTION, and CARE for THE BRIDE, and he makes said declaration in the sight of GOD and MOTHER JACKSON."

I looked up at her. "Karen," I asked, "will you be my wife?"

"Yes," she said.

I stood up. "Mother, will you witness this document?"

"Amen!" Mother exclaimed.

She signed her name, "Mother Erma Jackson," and I added: "the First Day of Spring, the 21st day of March, in the year of our Lord 1987."

We dined that night on the tastiest chicken dinner I had ever eaten. After supper I gave Karen the Bible and we lit the large oil lamp. I explained to her that in Bible times a Jewish girl who was engaged lit an oil lamp and placed it in her window, until the bridegroom came with his friends and called her to come to the wedding. She promised to keep it lit in her window until we were married. Then we played Mother Jackson's favorite song, "Jesus Dropped the Charges." We sang and laughed and celebrated.

Then Karen revealed to me their secret. Two weeks before I had asked Mother and Karen to have dinner with me on my birthday, Mother had awakened early one morning singing and praising God. Karen woke up, and asked her why she was so happy.

"I'm always happy," she chuckled.

"I know. But something's going on. Come on. Tell me."

"Okay. But it's a secret," Mother agreed.

"I won't tell anyone," Karen replied eagerly.

"You promise?" Mother asked.

"Yes, I promise. What is it?"

"You know how I've been praying for the Lord to give you a husband before I die and go home to Jesus?" Mother said.

"Yes," Karen said cautiously.

"Well, the Lord woke me up this morning and told me who it is."

"He did?"

"Yes, He did."

"Well, who is it?" whispered Karen.

Mother looked at her. "David Davis." There was a silence as Karen considered the possibility.

"Well, there's nothing going on between us now," Karen stated calmly.

They agreed together not to share it with anyone and to wait and see what the Lord would do.

It was two weeks later that God spoke to me. I looked at Mother. Now I understood. "So that's why you were so quiet that night."

"O-o-oh," she said, "I couldn't talk. The Holy Ghost put a holy hush on my mouth. I couldn't talk, so I just sat back and watched Him work. God is so-o-o good. First, He gives me a Jewish daughter, and then He throws you in for good measure!"

The next day I called our pastor.

"Pastor," I said, "I am in love with Karen Janeway, and she is in love with me. I think we're supposed to get married."

"I know," the pastor responded. "God told me. I was just waiting for you and Karen to hear. I think it should be soon. You two don't have any time to waste. I'll meet with you and we'll make arrangements."

Two months later, on a Saturday morning, I donned my tuxedo again. I was going to marry Karen. That morning there was a rainstorm. Ben Harney came to pick me up in a car. We dashed through the rain in ankle-high puddles to pick up flowers before we headed for Brooklyn. The rain poured as we drove through the Brooklyn-Battery Tunnel. We prayed for the rain to stop. The wedding was going to be held outside in the pastor's backyard in Seagate, an Orthodox Jewish neighborhood next to Coney Island. As we arrived at the house, the rain let up a little, but still continued.

Just as the service began, the rain stopped. A beautiful rainbow appeared over Seagate as the guests gathered on the lawn. Ben and I walked out and stood with the pastor. Many of my friends, colleagues, and students were there. My younger brother and his wife drove up from Baltimore. The worship team started to sing from an upstairs balcony overlooking the backyard. Then the ushers, including my old friend Charley, rolled a white runner up the driveway and across the lawn to where we stood. The singers sang, "We've Come to Praise Him," and many joined them. Two little flower girls, both named Joy, one black and one white, walked up the runner and rounded the corner of the house. Then came Karen's bridesmaid, Amy, another Jewish believer. Finally Karen appeared, escorted by her father. She looked glorious! Even breathtaking! Her father, who had flown in from Detroit with Karen's stepmother, handed his daughter to me.

From behind we heard music. We turned to see Noel Pointer standing on the roof playing his electric blue violin and singing, "Amazing grace, how sweet the sound that saved a wretch like me...." Ben handed me his handkerchief.

The pastor asked us to make our vows to each other. Karen turned to me, and said these words:

> "David, I promise in the sight of God and my family and friends, to honor and serve you as my husband as long as I live. I recognize that even as God has given you to me as that good and perfect gift, that it is a gift which is truly a calling—a calling to stand behind you and with you in actions, in words, perhaps above all in prayer, to go to God daily on your behalf that you might become all that God has

ordained you to be. I vow to go before God continually, that He might fill me to overflowing with His divine and unconditional love for you—and that even in times of testing I will stand in faith on the Word of God that no weapon formed against us and our union shall prosper."

People all over the yard were sobbing. An Orthodox Jew in a black hat was hanging over the fence, watching and listening. I read my covenant vow to Karen again—the vow I had read the night I had proposed. The yard was a sea of handkerchiefs and Kleenex. The pastor pronounced us man and wife. As we kissed, a roar of "Hallelujahs" arose.

Later that day, during the celebration, Karen sang a song she wrote, "Surely Goodness and Mercy Shall Follow Me." I testified about how God had arrested this Ph.D. and actor. Karen's brother David, the musician/psychiatrist, brought his keyboard and played Duke Ellington's "Come Sunday" as a gift to his sister. Karen's father told her that it was the best wedding he had ever attended.

– Chapter 4 –

Times Square Church

We began living in my Greenwich Village apartment, but it wasn't mine anymore. It was ours. At Karen's suggestion, I repainted the apartment photographer's white, so the colors she was about to add would be more dramatic. My life as a bachelor was finished. The old "macho" browns and earth tones were replaced with rich burgundies, blues, and golds. Our home became a subtle symphony of color. My artist wife had created a whole new environment for us.

Soon after we were married, I had a dream about us. Karen and I were sitting at a long table filled with young people. I thought perhaps that the dream was indicating that we should look for a larger apartment in Brooklyn and that Mother should live with us. But then the Lord provided her with a perfect, little studio apartment on West 71st Street. She was delighted with it, and we had a lot of fun fixing it up with her. Still I didn't understand the dream, but our lives were changing.

As the fall semester started at the university, I became more and more dissatisfied with my work. I was the chairman of a performing arts program founded upon the principles of secular humanism. It was now difficult to teach Henrik Ibsen or Tennessee Williams when I disagreed with what they said. As we taught our students to think, perform, and create, we enthroned the god of SELF. For me, it was beginning to be, as Macbeth said, all so much "sound and fury, signifying nothing." I wanted to do the best job I could, but I disagreed with much of what we were doing.

Karen decided to leave her job at Charles Jourdan. She wasn't comfortable working in the Fifth Avenue showroom modeling shoes in seductive, short skirts anymore. She began to devote herself to her music, playing the piano and writing songs to the Lord. She loved to rehearse with the worship team and sing to the Lord. These anointed singers and musicians were writing new songs and began to work on their first recording.

Some music team members wrote a musical based on the Book of Daniel, which they hoped to bring to Broadway. I acted and Karen sang in it. We performed the premier at a big church in Washington, D.C., my hometown. The cast and crew were hosted by local Christians in their homes, and Karen and I stayed with a lovely, elderly black woman, Martha Jones. There in her apartment memories of my childhood flooded my thoughts.

My grandfather, a prominent Washington attorney, worked for the Carnegie Endowment for International Peace. As a child I visited my grandparents' mansion in the suburbs, and I loved to play in the servants' quarters. They had a black maid named Izola whom I really liked. Even as a child I was puzzled by the racist and anti-Semitic remarks that I heard at home. Though I didn't understand why, I felt there was something wrong with such attitudes. Now I understood that God had created us in His image and there was truly no difference between us. Here, Karen and I were staying in a poor section of the nation's capital with this humble, black woman who slept on the couch so she could give us her bed. Martha Jones showed us a big black King James Bible, which she stroked lovingly and called her "honey." She said she had bought it years ago on an installment plan of one dollar a week.

I remembered how upset Izola was when my mother died. I called my aunt to see if I could locate Izola. She said that Izola lived in a nursing home, and so I telephoned her. When I told her who I was she was delighted. I explained to her how I had met Jesus, and she said that she too was a believer and had prayed for us for years.

Other memories of Washington came back to me. My father, an historian, was a Bureau Chief at the National Archives. From the big, open windows of his Pennsylvania Avenue office I watched the inaugural parade of President Dwight D. Eisenhower when I was a boy.

My father was a practicing Roman Catholic as I was growing up, but in the last years of his life he regularly attended the Full Gospel Business Men's meetings. Some years before I met the Lord, he even took me to one such meeting.

Across the Potomac River at Arlington Cemetery, I remembered standing on a hill while a Marine Corps honor guard fired a 21-gun salute as they buried my older brother, Pat. A young officer handed my mother the folded

American flag they had just taken from my brother's casket. She clasped the flag to her bosom as a lone trumpet played "Taps." Those were the days of the Vietnam War. While many college students were busy dodging the draft and protesting U.S. involvement in the war, Pat died in a training accident. He was trying to save two of his men from a hand grenade, as they prepared for Vietnam. Later, my college roommate was buried nearby—another casualty of the war.

I recalled directing Eugene O'Neill's "Long Days Journey Into Night" at the Kennedy Center for the Performing Arts. I had also acted in "A Soldier's Play" at Ford's Theatre, where Abraham Lincoln was assassinated by an actor who hated him for freeing the slaves.

Martha Jones invited a young friend to dinner after the Sunday morning service. Karen Clark had been the director of a large church choir. One day during a meeting, just after the choir had finished singing, an old lady stood up and began to sing the simple melody, "Hallelujah." All over the church people were healed. Karen Clark said she wanted that kind of anointing. As a teacher in an inner city school, her heart ached for the teenage girls and boys whose lives so desperately needed to be touched by the love and power of God. However, the Lord told her that it would cost her everything. Little by little he began to strip away the things of this world. She resigned as choir director and was now preparing to go to Africa as a missionary.

Karen Clark asked if she could pray for us. First, she prayed for Karen, and she had a strong word concerning how the Lord would use her in worship. Then, as she prayed for me, she stopped and looked at me. "God is going to do a quick work," she said. "He is going to put a burning inside you that will drive you to the place He wants you to go. He has a very specific work for you to do. Don't resist. Go." I knew it was the word of the Lord to me.

Karen and I flew to California to spend the New Year's holiday and to visit my sister. I got the flu and that was when I really started to hear from God. He told me a major change was coming. We took my sister to a service at Church on the Way in North Hollywood where Pastor Jack Hayford preached. When he finished, he said that if anyone wanted to receive Jesus he or she could simply go to one of the prayer rooms and someone would pray with him or her. In tears, my sister looked at me and said, "I want to go to one of those rooms. Will you take me over there?" I walked with her to a prayer room where she received Jesus.

As we flew back to New York, Karen concurred with what I felt the Lord was saying to me. Again and again she said, "I don't know what's happening. I've got such a churning inside of me. I feel like a big change is about to happen. A very big change."

Soon after our holiday we heard that David Wilkerson had returned to New York to start a church. I didn't know much about David Wilkerson but I did know that he had written the book, *The Cross and the Switchblade*, which had been made into a movie. He also had been very successful in rehabilitating drug addicts. His new congregation, Times Square Church, held its meetings at Town Hall in Times Square. I wanted to hear David Wilkerson speak. I invited my friend Charley to attend a meeting with us and hoped my friend would be freed from alcohol. He didn't come, but his wife did.

As the three of us sat in the meeting, David Wilkerson preached and Karen wept. She cried throughout the entire meeting. Charley's wife tried not to notice. During the subway ride home, Karen still couldn't hold back the tears. People stared at her, and I put my arm around her to comfort her. When we arrived home, I asked her what had happened. All she could say was that the hand of God had come upon her during the meeting, and it had shattered her beyond words.

Shortly thereafter, Times Square Church moved into the Nederlander Theatre on 41st Street, between 7th and 8th Avenues. That block is known as "Crack Alley," because the police don't bother the addicts who prowl the street there, some of whom live in cardboard boxes. The Nederlander is the re-named historic Billy Rose Theatre, where many famous plays were once produced. Some of my friends had worked there, but now, because of the drug and crime epidemic, it couldn't be rented as a theatre anymore. Next door to the theatre was a transvestite bar.

A year earlier, David Wilkerson was walking through Times Square when a drug pusher stopped him. "Crack" was becoming popular in drug circles at that time. The pusher asked, "Hey man, do you want to buy some of the stuff that killed Lennie Bias?" Lennie Bias was the best college basketball player in America. After signing a multimillion dollar contract with the Boston Celtics, he went to a party at the University of Maryland, where he died from an overdose of "crack." David Wilkerson stood in Times Square with tears in his eyes. At that moment the Holy Spirit told him to leave his home in Texas and move to New York. There, God said He would give him a Broadway Theatre to raise up a testimony to Jesus right in the middle of the drugs, crime, prostitution, and pornography.

One night, I went to a meeting at the Nederlander alone. After David Wilkerson preached, I answered the altar call and asked the Lord for direction. Pastor Wilkerson looked at me from the stage and said, "God's all over you, son." The next Saturday morning I returned to the theatre because I had heard that they had started an outreach to street people. A dozen or more young men of God from different parts of America had come to New York to help "Brother Dave," as they called him. Some of them were living in the dressing rooms of the theatre.

That day there were about thirty of us. One brother said he believed that we should pray against the spirit of suicide and we did. Then we went out two by two onto the streets of Times Square. My partner and I talked to a drug addict named Paul in the Port Authority Bus terminal. I bought him a cup of coffee. Then I laid hands on him and prayed for him. I told him to come to the meeting the next night at the Nederlander and that we would try to get him into a rehabilitation program.

Several hours later we all regathered at the theatre. A white, teenage boy from New Jersey reported that he had descended into a subway station and tapped an old black man on the shoulder. As the man turned to him, the boy told him that Jesus loved him. Just then the train roared into the station. The man said he had planned to jump under the train and kill himself.

The next night, Karen and I attended the Sunday evening service at Times Square Church. It was crowded, and we sat in the balcony. On the music team there were four or five singers and a few musicians, including a trumpet player who had just been released from jail. As the worship began, I could see that Karen was moved. David Wilkerson preached another powerful sermon. I was watching a man who had God's heart for the lost. Again, Karen wept through the whole message.

When David Wilkerson gave the altar call many people came forward. I had been praying for Paul and was sure he would be there, but I didn't see him. I stood up in the balcony and scanned the people standing in front of the stage. He wasn't there. David Wilkerson started to pray and then stopped. Paul was walking down the aisle of the theatre. Pastor Wilkerson called him up on the stage. He said, "There's conviction all over you. Do you want to get free from drugs?"

"Yes," said Paul.

After praying for him, Pastor Wilkerson encouraged him. "We're going to send you to a program. Come on back—we have some brothers who can help you." Paul walked backstage.

Now, I was crying. There I was, standing in a Broadway theatre like so many in which I had worked, but now, here in this theatre, a young man was getting a chance for a new life. This was not about applause or fame or money. This was about changed lives. This was impacting society. I wanted to be a part of it. I dropped into my seat stunned.

After the service, the people were leaving the theatre but we just sat there. Finally I said, "Honey, this is our church."

Karen was disturbed. "What about our other congregation?" she asked. "We got married there. They're our family. I'm on the worship team. We have a recording coming out. This church is going to be so big, we'll never even meet the pastor. I'll probably never sing again," she pleaded.

"Come on, honey. Let's go home," I said, not wanting to force the issue at that moment. "Everybody's gone. They're turning out the lights. We'll get locked in here. We have to go."

"I can't," she said.

"What do you mean?" I asked.

"I don't know. I just can't get up."

Finally, I pried her out of the seat and helped her toward the exit. There was hardly anyone left in the theatre. As we entered the lobby, we walked into another couple leaving the theatre. It was David Wilkerson and his wife. "Hello, I'm David Wilkerson," he said. "This is my wife Gwen." He reached out and shook my hand.

"I'm David Davis, and this is my wife Karen."

He looked at me and responded, "I've seen you before— you're hungry for God. What do you do?" I told him. Then as he looked at us he asked, "What's the division between you two?"

Wondering how he could know about us, I answered, "Well, we're seeking the Lord's will for what congregation we should attend."

Then Karen added, "We're part of another fellowship, and…"

He put a hand on each of our shoulders and prayed, "Oh Lord, You show them."

As we all stepped onto 41st Street, he stopped and asked, "You said you work in the theatre?"

"Yes."

"Are you free Friday morning? Could you come over here and help me set up the stage? I don't know anything about theatres."

"Yes, I'm free," I replied.

"Good," he said. "10:00 a.m., okay? See you then."

I wanted to know more about the Wilkersons so I bought *The Cross and the Switchblade* and read it. I was touched by David Wilkerson's obedience, courage, and compassion for the lost. God had moved with such miraculous power through one obedient young pastor. I so wanted God to use me and asked Him to forgive me for wasting so much of my life. I said to Karen, "David Wilkerson is in his late fifties, and has served God since he was eight. Why didn't God come and get me earlier?"

When I read Gwen Wilkerson's book, *In His Strength*, I couldn't put it down and finished it in one night. In it she described her battles with cancer. She revealed the struggles that she and David had encountered in their marriage as she coped with David's fame and absences, but also how the Lord had dramatically saved their marriage.

That Friday I met "Brother Dave" at the theatre. We walked through Times Square trying to buy large safety pins to fasten the curtains on the stage. I showed him the plaque at the spot where Eugene O'Neill was born in a hotel in Times Square. I told him that O'Neill, considered America's greatest playwright, had cursed God with his final breath. We stood in Schubert Alley, and I pointed to the location where a Broadway theatre had been knocked down to build a gigantic luxury hotel. Actors tried in vain to stop the wrecking crew and the police arrested some of them. As the wrecking ball hit the theatre, actors and actresses stood on 44th Street crying. "They wouldn't do that for Jesus," said Brother Dave.

After having lunch at Beefsteak Charlie's, we returned to the theatre. We finished moving chairs and platforms around on the stage. Brother Dave asked me if I knew any believers who could run the lights and sound. "They need to be on fire for Jesus," he explained. "Everyone who works here needs to be a Levite. This is God's house."

I told him I knew a young lady attending the church who was a lighting designer and that I would look for a sound man.

Karen and I made an appointment to see the pastor and elders of the congregation we'd been attending. We thanked them for everything they had done for us. We had come to know Jesus, had grown in our walk with Him, and had been married there. I told them I believed we were being called to Times Square Church, and I showed them the Scripture the Lord had given me from Isaiah 30:20-21a (NKJ):

> "And though the Lord gives you
> The bread of adversity and the
>   water of affliction,
> Yet your teachers will not be moved into a
>   corner anymore,
> But your eyes shall see your teachers.
> Your ears shall hear a word behind you,
>   saying, 'This is the way, walk in it.' "

"I believe I need older, mature men over me to teach me and be examples," I said, "and David Wilkerson and his leadership team are those men."

The pastor looked at me and responded, "I believe this is the word of the Lord to you. We love you both very much, and we'll miss you dearly. You have my blessing." We all prayed, and Karen and I walked out of the music studio and down the steps onto 41st Street. We ran the two blocks to the Nederlander, where a service was just beginning.

Not long after this Pastor Dave approached me in the theatre. "Have you found a sound man?" he asked.

"Well, the fellow I found isn't really walking with the Lord," I answered him. "I don't think he's the right guy."

He looked at me and said, "You do it."

"But I don't know anything about sound," I protested.

"You can learn," he replied, and walked away.

I stood in the back of this Broadway theatre and thought, *I direct plays in theatres like this. I hire sound men and fire them when they don't give me what I want.* But I did it. Sitting in the back of the sanctuary, behind a huge console with all kinds of controls I didn't understand, I became the Times Square Church sound man. The worship leader who had set up the system tried to help me. During services, whenever something went wrong with the sound, people turned around and looked at me. Embarrassment provides great motivation to improve. God was moving in the meetings in such a powerful way that sometimes I closed my eyes and raised my hands and just worshiped the Lord. Suddenly, I would remember that I was the sound man and try to figure out what to do next.

I also took notes on all the messages I heard. Each

morning following a service I made a cup of coffee, went over my notes, and transferred them into a large notebook. I still have that stack of notebooks, filled with rich spiritual insights.

One evening, David Wilkerson asked us to join him for dinner. We met in a restaurant on Columbus Avenue and West 68th Street, four blocks from Karen's old apartment. As we ate, he asked Karen if she was working. She had quit her job in the fashion business and had been thinking of looking for something else. He explained that he was looking for someone to type and edit his newsletter, which was distributed to half a million people every three weeks. When we finished the meal he suggested that we walk to his office.

In those days the Times Square Church office was on Broadway and 69th Street. We took the elevator up to the second floor. Brother Dave showed Karen a desk with a typewriter on it. "This will be your desk," he said. "I'll give you my notes from one of my messages and you'll type them into the form of a newsletter." Then he turned to me and said, "You have a call on your life."

"What should I do?" I asked, "Go to Bible school?"

"No. Just sit under the teaching in the church. If you're faithful, God will use you," he replied. He picked up two shopping bags and said, "Come here, you'll need these." He started to peruse the bookshelves in his office and in the hallway, taking books off the shelves and putting them in the bags. He looked at one and said, *"Miller's Church History*—the best."

We walked back onto Broadway. "Can you start Monday?" he asked Karen. "Yes," she responded.

"Good. Goodnight."

Karen and I sat on the subway looking at each other.

She had a job working for David Wilkerson, and I had a Bible school in two shopping bags.

On Sunday nights, Karen sat in Times Square Church and heard David Wilkerson preach under the anointing of the Holy Spirit. Then on Monday mornings he gave her his handwritten sermon notes. She sat at her desk with a giant print King James Bible to doublecheck his Scripture references and typed his notes into newsletter form. The Word of God was being richly deposited into my wife's spirit.

Karen worked under Barbara Mackery, who had been Brother Dave's executive assistant for nearly twenty years. Barb and Karen became close friends. Her husband Jimmy, who is legally deaf and blind, worked next to me at the sound board. Using high-powered earphones, he taped and duplicated the messages for distribution around the world. On his own, Jimmy had been hit by cars three different times; now he walked the streets of New York with his golden retriever, seeing-eye dog, "Mr. Bowser."

Gwen Wilkerson helped in the office by answering mail while her husband was alone with God receiving his next message. Barb's sister Gayle also worked on the office staff. The ladies in the office frequently ministered to afflicted people who telephoned the office. Karen was being trained in the ways of God as she watched and listened to these godly women. Occasionally, they would all jump in a taxi at lunch time and go to a Charles Jourdan sample sale. They would return with fine leather shoes, bags, or belts they had purchased for five dollars.

One night, while I was running the sound system for the weekly worship rehearsal at the theatre, Karen met me after work. She was sitting next to me watching Barb, Gayle, and several other singers and musicians rehearse on the stage. After awhile, I realized that someone was standing in the aisle next to me. I turned around and saw Brother Dave. We greeted each other. After a few moments he asked Karen, "Do you sing?"

"Yes," she said, quite startled.

"Go up there and sing something," he encouraged her. He walked her down to the stage and told the others that Karen was going to sing a song. She climbed up on the stage, sat down at the grand piano, and adjusted the microphone that I was controlling from the back of the theatre. She began to play and sing a song she had written based on Psalm 139:

> "Search me, O God, and know my heart;
> Try me and know my thoughts.
> See if there be any hurtful way
> And lead me in the way everlasting.
>
> Take away the sin from my life
> Show me what is wrong and what is right.
> Teach me to be true to You
> In everything I do."

When she finished there was silence. "Stay up there and rehearse with them," Brother Dave said. "Start singing with the worship team on Sunday." Then he left.

Some weeks earlier, Karen had cried in this theatre because she thought she'd never sing again. That Sunday she began praising God on a Broadway stage where the Holy Spirit had begun to move in great power.

The Lord was systematically taking me out of show business, and my desire to act was dying. One day I went to an audition for a Pepsi commercial in the offices of a plush advertising agency. As I sat there looking at all the "beautiful people" who desperately wanted to do this commercial, I assessed the scene. "This is all about sex and selling. What am I doing here?"

Just then they called my name. I walked over to the receptionist and said, "I just quit."

"What?" she asked, astonished. I turned around and walked out of the office. I stepped onto 57th Street and felt released. It was my last audition for anything.

A short time later, after I had been running the sound system for about six months, Brother Dave approached me backstage and tossed a cassette tape to me. "Let me know what you think of this," he said.

Alone in our Village apartment I started the tape. A haunting shofar blast, a call, a summons opened John Thompson's *El Shaddai*. The shofar, the ram's horn, was used by the ancient priests of Israel to call God's chosen people to Himself. This musical compiled the stories of Abraham, Moses, and Mary's lamentation at the cross over Jesus' death, and culminated in a glorious, musical score describing the resurrected Lord.

When I heard the scene in which Abraham offers up his only son, Isaac, as a sacrifice, I fell on my knees in the middle of our living room floor and cried. The anointing of the Holy Spirit descended upon me and filled the apartment.

The next day I spoke with David Wilkerson. "Brother Dave," I said, "this piece is so anointed, I think we should do the whole thing right here in the theatre."

"So do we," he agreed. "One of the pastors was so moved listening to it in his car that he had to pull over to the side of the road. We'd like you to direct it. So make your arrangements and give me a budget," he instructed.

God had since provided a sound man who knew what he was doing. Now I was actually going to direct on Broadway for God! John Thompson, the composer, had moved to New York to be part of the church and had brought his sound equipment, including all kinds of synthesizers. John was the musical director, and his wife Patty sang the part of Mary. Ben Harney played Moses, and I played Abraham. We held auditions for singers, out of which the Times Square Church choir was born. Karen, of course, sang in the musical.

The production played to standing room only audiences, and we decided to add an extra performance. Hundreds of people, including a rabbi's wife, received Jesus at the altar calls we made each night.

Something profound was also happening to me. At the end of the musical I said these lines:

> "Now El Shaddai is calling for a remnant of holy people to throw off all that is impure, and to arise out of a corrupt generation and reflect His glory. He calls us to be that remnant. He calls for us to declare His righteousness; and by faith in the blood of the Lamb, we will arise...we will walk blameless before our God."

I realized I was no longer acting. I wasn't trying to be Abraham. I was speaking directly from my heart, but it wasn't just me. For the first time, I experienced the anointing of the Holy Spirit, as I proclaimed these words of truth.

The church began to have a burden for the Jewish people. Many Jewish believers were coming to the services. One elderly, Jewish man said he had prayed for fifty years for God to raise up a congregation in Manhattan that would care about the Jewish people. There are more Jews in the New York City area than in Israel. As Jewish believers came to the church, I introduced them to David Wilkerson. One time, he was talking to a couple visiting from Texas. The lady told him that the Jews didn't want Jesus. "Here's six who do," I said, and I introduced her to the Jewish believers standing next to me.

People of all races came to the church, too. The first four or five weddings at Times Square Church were interracial marriages between blacks and whites. They were a beautiful, genuine expression of the "one new man," reconciled "in one body through the cross" (Eph. 2:15-16, NKJ).

Each week between four hundred and five hundred people would pour into the theatre after work for the evening Bible studies. The first series was "The Call to Holiness." Through it we learned about the holiness of God and the practical steps to living an overcoming life. Believers who had known the Lord for many years said they had never heard such deep teaching. The roots of Christ-like character were penetrating deep into the hearts of those who were yielding to His Word. I was filled with wonderful spiritual food, and my stack of notebooks continued to grow.

On Friday nights, the church held prayer meetings. We prayed for revival in New York City, as well as for the nations, particularly Israel and China. One Friday evening, as we came out of the Times Square subway station on our way to the Nederlander, the irony of the change in my life struck me. "On Friday nights I used to get drunk," I told Karen. "Now we're going to a theatre to pray!"

One time Gary Wilkerson, David's oldest son, shared from the Word of God before we prayed. Gary was the baby born in *The Cross and the Switchblade*, and is now a pastor. As he spoke, I noticed Brother Dave was sitting in the front row with an open Bible, listening intently to Gary preach. "Look, he's teachable," I said to Karen, very impressed by his humility. "He's learning from his son."

As I continued to hear David Wilkerson's uncompromising messages and watch his life, I realized the truth of the apostle Paul's statement: "For though you might have ten thousand instructors in Christ, yet you do not have many fathers" (1 Cor. 4:15 NKJ). It was a privilege to be mentored by a man who carried God's heart for the afflicted. His love for God, and his broken heart over how God is dishonored and His truth is trampled served as powerful examples to me.

– Chapter 5 –

The Upper Room

Just one block from the Nederlander Theatre, the church rented the second floor of an old building on the corner of 41st Street and 8th Avenue, facing the huge, central bus station. We named it "The Upper Room." Now there was a testimony to Jesus on both ends of "Crack Alley." From the large window, the Sodom-like atmosphere of Times Square could be seen. Every Saturday we took groups out to the streets and invited needy people to the Upper Room for afternoon meetings. Volunteers served them coffee and sandwiches and gave them good clothes. Most importantly, we shared the gospel with them—the good news that they could have a new life and that there was a way out of their hopelessness.

Groups came from all over the country to be part of what God was doing in Times Square. Once I was put on a team with a very large, white man from Louisiana. We started to talk to a black addict who was sitting on the sidewalk outside the bus terminal. He protested, "It's not my fault. It's the cops' fault."

My partner got out his wallet and took out a card. He showed it to the pathetic man sitting on the sidewalk and asked him, "What's that say?"

The addict read out loud: "Cops for Christ."

"That's right; I'm a cop for Christ," the Louisiana man said. "And I love you, man. Come on, let me help you up. We're gonna give you some food and some hope." He pulled him up, and we took him across the street to the Upper Room.

One day, the leader of the Upper Room asked me to preach on the following Saturday. In graduate school, I had studied Speech Pedagogy and Aristotle's Five Canons of Rhetoric. I had even taught Public Speaking and had prepared lectures for twenty years. I knew how to give a speech. But now I needed help. I asked the Lord to show me how to preach. I knew if there was no anointing of the Holy Spirit, there would be no genuine results. One night as I prayed and sought the Lord alone in the dark of our apartment, I took out a pad of paper and a pen. After some time, I wrote something on the pad. I turned on a lamp and read four, large words: "SHOW THEM MY SON."

That Saturday morning, as I rode on the subway on my way uptown to Times Square, I surveyed the people in the subway car. I saw a man in a suit holding a briefcase on his lap—*probably a Wall Street broker*, I thought. Sitting next to him, was a woman carrying two Macy's shopping bags loaded with purchases. At the end of the car was a "bag lady," talking to herself or to someone who was not there. She was just one of the legions of women living on the streets of New York who carried all her possessions in bags. On my lap was my leather shoulder bag containing my Bible. I had the distinct impression that I was carrying something explosive—like dynamite—in my bag.

When I arrived, the Upper Room was packed with the outcasts of New York City. I took my place behind the pulpit and I looked out the window. My eyes rested on the back of the very same theatre where my actors' dream had come true several years prior to this moment. There I had stood on that stage on a Friday night listening to the "bravos." God in His mercy had rescued me. As I thought of His goodness to me, it was almost too much to bear. I had trouble speaking as I began to preach from Galatians 6:14 (NKJ): "But God forbid that I should boast except in the cross of our Lord Jesus Christ, by whom the world has been crucified to me, and I to the world."

I think I spoke for about fifteen or twenty minutes. When I finished, I invited any who did not know Jesus to come forward and I would pray for them. I closed my eyes and prayed silently in the Spirit. Before the meeting I had asked the Lord to save one soul. When I opened my eyes there were three people in front of me, kneeling and weeping.

Each Saturday when I returned home from the Upper Room, I immediately removed my clothes, put them in the laundry basket, and took a shower. The drug addicts, prostitutes, homeless, and AIDS victims had open sores on their bodies and carried an unmistakable odor. It was the smell of death.

Then Karen and I would have our dinner together. Excitedly, I would tell her of the day's miracles. "You've been blessed to receive so much," she said one day. "It's great that now you're giving out." She was right. She saw from week to week that God was subtly changing my heart, remolding it to feel as He felt and to see these broken lives as He saw them. He was giving me His burden and His heart for the lost.

One time I sat at a table in the Upper Room with a huge black man named David who was known for his violence. For some reason the ladies who worked in the Upper Room brought all the tough guys to me. I had developed a practice in working with street people that, when in doubt, I would use Luke 15, "The Prodigal Son." I gave David a Bible, opened it to Luke 15, and asked him to read Jesus' story of the lost son. He stared at the Bible, then back at me. Something was happening to this giant sitting across from me. I watched as his tough exterior began to crack and tears rolled down his face. "What is it, David?" I asked.

After a long pause, he looked down at the table. "I can't read," he said.

"Here, let me read it to you," I offered gently. He listened attentively as I read the story.

When I finished he said, "That's me, isn't it?"

"Yes, and it was me too. But Jesus changed me and He can change you as well," I explained. "I was an alcoholic but Jesus set me free. He can deliver you from your anger and pain." I prayed with this dejected man. We later made arrangements for David to start a reading program.

All week long I eagerly waited for Saturdays. I longed to reach out to lonely, hurting people and to share the good news with them. Teaching university theatre students, many of whom had come to New York seeking fame and fortune for themselves, had lost its attraction for me.

The church rented an old, three-story house on the Lower East Side of Manhattan in a very rough neighborhood. They called it "Timothy House." Some of the single brothers who had come to New York to be part of the church lived there. The house also became a residential rehabilitation (rehab) center for addicts and alcoholics.

The director of the program asked me to teach the residents there. What a joy and a privilege it was to prepare lessons on the reality of "How to Overcome Anger," or "The Authority of God's Word," instead of trying to teach student actors to appear "real" on stage or in front of a TV camera.

The majority of the men at Timothy House were young. Most heroin addicts die by the time they reach the age of forty. I heard many tragic and painful stories as I became acquainted with the men. One older man, who came to Timothy House through the Upper Room, told me that he had been living in Central Park under the bushes. I noticed that his shoes were falling apart, so I brought him a pair of mine. Once he came up to me in the church and said, "Look, Brother David, new shoes for my new walk with Jesus!"

At another drug rehab center in Connecticut I preached on John 14:18: "I will not leave you orphans...." After an altar call and prayer time, a young fellow came to me. "Brother David," he asked, "do you remember me?"

"Yes, I do, but I hardly recognize you."

"I met you at the Upper Room," he said, "and you all sent me to Timothy House. Now I'm here." This handsome young man continued, "I'm an orphan, but I know now that God is my Father." He had been a derelict on the streets, but here he stood healthy and beaming.

Karen was asked to sing at the Upper Room. Since I was going to preach that day on "The Lamb of God," she sang about the gift of love we had crucified, and how the world had mocked Him as He died for us. The room resonated with the love of the Lamb of God as Karen pleaded in song for Jesus to wash us in His precious blood and make us lambs of God.

After the meeting our friend Greg, the keyboard player, came up to us and said, "You know, you guys are a team." We'd never really thought of ourselves that way.

God poured out His Spirit in the Upper Room, and hundreds came to the Lord. It was wonderful to see how the Lord was working. We had started going out on the streets two by two. He provided a place to bring the needy. Now there was another place for them to live. We did not despise the day of small beginnings, and as we were faithful with a little, the Lord provided more.

It was at this time that I had a dream, which I wrote down in my spiritual diary:

> "David Wilkerson and I were standing on the top of the highest building in Manhattan. We were outside on a flat roof. Before us was a sumptuous spread of food laid on a long table. The food was the most delectable that I had ever tasted—a myriad of beautiful colors and wonderful aromas. We were sampling it and it was free. 'Here, try this,' Brother Dave said and handed me something delicious to eat.
>
> "Then I heard the voice of God say to me, 'David, where do you think I want you to work?'
>
> "I looked down at New York City and answered, 'Here, in New York.'
>
> "'No,' He said and He turned my head to see what appeared to me to be San Francisco Bay."

The dream ended. As I wrote it in my diary, I felt I understood most of it. The wonderful food was the pure

Word of God I had been receiving at Times Square Church, where Pastor Dave had been feeding and nurturing me through his messages. However, I had no idea why God seemed to want me to work for Him in San Francisco.

– Chapter 6 –

The Call

In the summer of 1988, Karen and I took a two-week vacation to Israel. Although she is Jewish, Karen had never been to Israel, and I wanted her to see it. As we approached our destination, the plane banked, and we saw the shoreline of Israel below us. Tears streamed down Karen's face as she got her first glimpse of the land of her inheritance. From Ben Gurion Airport we drove up to Jerusalem. It was clear to me that something very significant was happening in my wife's heart. Not being Jewish myself, I didn't understand it all, but I tried.

I took Karen to the places where I had met with the Lord. We spent quiet hours in the presence of the Lord at the Garden Tomb and at the Garden of Gethsemane on the Mount of Olives. We went to the "Shepherds' Field" outside of Bethlehem. Boaz and Ruth, and David lived there and it is near the place where Jesus was born. In a little chapel there, Karen sang in the Spirit, and the glory of the Lord filled the place. I was watching my wife blossom.

At Yad V'shem, the memorial to the victims of the Holocaust, we were horrified. One special building is dedicated to the Jewish children who died in the Holocaust. Descending into the dark, narrow corridor, we saw what appeared to be thousands of tiny, flickering candles, engulfed in blackness. I remembered God's promise to Abraham, "...look toward the heavens, and count the stars, if you are able to count them...So shall your descendants be" (Gen. 15:5). We stood silently, surrounded by these tiny lights that pierced the darkness. "Joshua, age four...David, age six," a voice called out. "...Daniel, age three...Sarah, age two..." It was an endless roll call of the names of children who had perished. We were devastated.

As we exited into the blazing sunlight, we stood on the Judean hills overlooking Jerusalem. We understood in a deeper way how the nation of Israel had been born out of the tragedy of the Holocaust. This living country was brought forth from the ashes of the cremated bodies of six million Jews. After two thousand years of wandering in exile, the Jews had come home.

Of course I called Frida, my Arab friend who had been healed from breast cancer. She immediately invited us to lunch. Karen and I walked through "the eye of the needle," the little gateway, into the courtyard beneath her home. What a joyous reunion! Frida looked so healthy, and Sabrina had grown and matured in the two years since I had been in Israel. Sabrina and Karen quickly became friends. We had a wonderful Arabic feast, and I gave Frida *The Cross and the Switchblade* to read. We made a date to meet with them again before we were scheduled to travel north to Galilee.

Several days later, we gathered again in their little sitting room in the Old City. Frida had read David Wilkerson's book, and she described how it had affected her. I told her about Times Square Church, and that I was working with drug addicts in the Upper Room and at Timothy House. Then Frida confided in us. "David, there are drugs all over the Old City. I am afraid to let Sabrina go out at night."

"Drugs? Here?" I asked. I was shocked. How could there be drugs in the Old City of Jerusalem—in the place where Jesus died and was raised from the dead? I could hardly believe it.

"Yes, it's terrible," she said. Then Frida asked me this question: "David, can you bring your church here?"

This Arab mother's plea for help pierced my heart like an arrow. As I sat there with my Jewish wife and three Arabs in Jerusalem, the Lord began to stir something deep inside me.

The next day, as we traveled north through Jericho and up the Jordan valley, I pondered what Frida had said. We stayed at the Scottish Hospice in Tiberias overlooking the Sea of Galilee and spent several precious days by the lake. We visited Capernaum and the Mount of Beatitudes. We feasted on "St. Peter's fish" sitting beside the sea where Jesus had called Peter and the others.

I bought a copy of Derek Prince's book, *Appointment in Jerusalem*, and began to read it. He tells the story of Lydia Christensen, a Danish school teacher who met Jesus in a dramatic way. She left a life of physical comfort and professional fulfillment in Denmark to travel alone to Jerusalem in 1928. There she founded and ran an orphanage for Arab and Jewish children. Derek Prince, while serving in Jerusalem in the British army, met Lydia and later married her. During the War of Independence in 1948, they lived in Jerusalem with their eight adopted daughters. As soon as I finished reading the book, I gave it to Karen. We both sensed God was speaking to us through Lydia's story and that we, too, had just had an "appointment in Jerusalem."

When we returned to New York, we couldn't escape the burning in our hearts for Israel and the drug problem there. Soon after our return, David Wilkerson preached on "The Joy of Spending." He spoke on Jesus' "Parable of the Talents" in Matthew 25, concerning how God gives us abilities and expects us to use them for Him. To those who do this the Lord says: "Well done, good and faithful servant; you were faithful over a few things, I will make you ruler over many things. Enter into the joy of your Lord" (Mt. 25:21 NKJ).

In his message, David Wilkerson talked about H.A. Baker and his wife, who labored for the Lord in Tibet and China for many years. The couple suffered many hardships in Tibet. They lived in a converted chicken coop, which Mrs. Baker decorated with little curtains. Mr. Baker made long, solitary excursions on foot to take the gospel to remote, mountain villages. When he returned his wife always placed a bouquet of fresh wild flowers on the table to welcome him home. At a time when the first Teen Challenge Center in Brooklyn was in financial trouble, they sent their life's savings to Brother Dave, and the money rescued the program.

Prior to preaching this message, Brother Dave had been away for a few days seeking the Lord. There was a powerful anointing on him as he spoke. He said that while he was gone the Lord told him that Times Square Church was to be a "sending church," and that there were people in the church whom God was setting apart to be sent. Then he gave an altar call. From opposite ends of the theatre, Karen and I met at the altar and grasped each other's hands. We knew God was confirming what we both felt so strongly.

Later that week, Brother Dave invited us to have dinner with him and his wife Gwen. As we sat in the restaurant eating, he said, "I heard Israel stole your heart. What happened over there?" I shared with them about our time in Israel.

He listened as I told him our story. When I finished, he looked at me. "God's calling you," he said. "You need to obey. We don't want you to go—we'll miss you. But you have to go. Make your preparations and we'll help you."

The fall semester was just beginning again at the university where I was a tenured, full professor. Even with this confirmation from our pastor, we weren't sure what to do next to prepare, except to pray. We started a prayer group for Israel. Although there were only a handful of us, the little group was faithful, and Karen and I felt tremendous support.

One day, I told Brother Dave I didn't think the church was praying enough for Israel. "We've just decided to start praying all night on Friday nights after our regular weekly prayer meeting," He responded. "We've been praying about who should run it. You do it."

We had some glorious times in those all night meetings! The Lord was training me in His school of prayer. We interceded for all the growing ministries of the church. The pastors; the choir; the children's and youth groups; the prison ministry; the Raven truck, which distributed food to the hungry; the Upper Room; and Timothy House were all on our agenda.

One time, at about three in the morning, there were twenty-five of us praying on the stage in the sanctuary. I felt we should pray for the altar call that would take place on Sunday morning, and I encouraged the prayer warriors to continue praying during the Sunday morning meeting. During that Sunday service, even before the preacher had finished his message, people streamed down the aisles, convicted of their sins. The minister looked surprised. Later he asked me, "Did you see that altar call?"

"Yes," I said. "We prayed for it, and the Lord heard our prayers."

At another all-night prayer meeting, in the early hours of the morning, I was praying for Israel and the drug addicts there, when a spirit of travail came upon me. I told the Lord I would go to Israel and build Him a house for Jewish and Arab drug addicts. I had been reading about King David's desire to build a house for the Lord. Nathan the prophet told King David, "Thus says the Lord, 'Are you the one who should build Me a house to dwell in?'…The Lord will make a house for you" (2 Sam. 7:5,11). I was rebuked for my pride, and I told the Lord how sorry I was. I thanked Him for His promise to build His own house. Then I prayed this Scripture to the Lord:

> "For Thou, O Lord of Hosts, the God of Israel, hast made a revelation to Thy servant, saying, 'I will build you a house'; therefore Thy servant has found courage to pray this prayer to Thee. And now, O Lord God, Thou art God, and Thy words are truth, and Thou hast promised this good thing to Thy servant" (2 Sam. 7:27-28).

Every time I asked the Lord to reconfirm that we were to move to Israel, He was faithful to do so. Once, while I was sitting in a service, I prayed: "Lord, confirm our call again in this message." The preacher said, "Please turn to Acts, Chapter Seven, verse three." Then he read: "Depart from your country and your relatives, and come into the land that I will show you." It was Abraham's call.

"All right, Lord," I confessed, "I hear You."

People came to Times Square Church from all over the world. Once, in a Sunday night meeting, David Wilkerson asked people in the congregation to call out the country from where they had come. "Korea...England...Germany..." and other countries were in the roll call. Then from the balcony we heard a voice thunder, "Jerusalem!"

"Karen, we need to meet that man," I said. We found him after the meeting and introduced ourselves. Leslie Moxham, an elderly man from Britain, pastored a congregation in Jerusalem. We ate dinner with Leslie and his wife Lilla and discussed our call to Israel. "David," he cautioned, "make sure you get it from the Word of God. Remember, 'Thy word is a lamp to my feet, and a light to my path' (Ps. 119:105)."

The Lord continued to confirm our call through the Scriptures. One particularly strong word to us was, "Behold, I and the children whom the Lord has given me are for signs and wonders in Israel" (Is. 8:18). I wasn't sure what it meant. We didn't have any children, but I wasn't going to argue with the Lord.

One night, Karen and I were having dinner in a coffee shop on Broadway. We talked about needing $300 to take an intensive course in basic Hebrew before we moved to Israel. We asked the Lord to give us one more sign that we should leave everything and go. We wanted to be totally sure that we weren't being swayed by our emotions or any romantic ideas that we might have had about Israel. Then Karen went to a music rehearsal in the Nederlander, and I went to a staff meeting at the Upper Room.

After the meeting, at about 10 p.m., I started to walk the one block up "Crack Alley" to the theatre to meet Karen. There were drug addicts everywhere, so I prayed quietly in the Spirit. Suddenly a well-dressed young man walked toward me. He stopped. "Oh, you're the one I'm looking for!" he said in a strange foreign accent that I couldn't place. "I've seen you in the church. You're going to Israel. Here, God told me to give you this." He reached in his pocket, thrust some money into my hands, and walked off. Two street people were watching this interaction just a few feet away. Quickly, I put the roll of bills into my pocket and continued to walk toward the theatre. Then I stopped and turned around. He was gone. I hurried up the block and entered the lobby of the theatre. I took the money out of my pocket and counted it. It was almost $300. I went up on stage and said to Karen, "We just got our sign." I told David Wilkerson. "Probably an angel!" he replied.

Although I was pleased to have started a Bible study at the university with several students who were believers, it became clear to me that I had to resign. As Karen and I prayed about it, we agreed that I should announce my resignation in January of 1989, and that we would move to Israel the following September. That way I could teach summer school and save more money.

I wrote a long resignation letter addressed to the President of Fordham University. He was a Jesuit priest and a friend of mine. In the letter, I poured out my feelings and beliefs, and tried to explain how my new life and relationship with Jesus were incompatible with my position at the university. I met with David Wilkerson and asked him to read my resignation letter. He read it silently, then returned it to me. "Do you want it straight?" he asked.

"Yes, sir," I said.

"It's too long and too preachy. Tell them what happened to you in one page," he advised. "Then pray for doors to open to testify about what God has done for you." Then he asked, "You've been there eighteen years?"

"Yes," I replied. He just stared at me.

As we parted on the corner of Broadway and 69th Street, he started to walk away and then called, "David."

"Yes, sir?" I answered.

"Don't forget to thank Jesus for your new heart!" He turned and left.

I stood on Broadway in the cold January night. I was crying so hard I didn't want to go into the subway, so instead I started walking down Broadway. I passed Lincoln Center for the Performing Arts where I worked and continued on toward Times Square. As I entered the theatre district, the neon lights were ablaze on the theatre marquees. I stopped and looked all around. It didn't mean anything to me anymore. It all seemed unreal. I continued walking through Times Square…with my new heart.

I took Brother Dave's advice, and re-wrote my resignation letter on one type-written page. In it I wrote: "I believe we are a world torn loose from our foundations, hurtling toward the abyss because we 'worship the creature rather than the Creator,' as the apostle Paul put it." I wrote that God had called me to "proclaim the truth that sets people free," and to "show them My Son."

Several days after I sent the letter to the President, his secretary called me to meet with him. As I entered his office he closed the door, which wasn't like him. I assumed he wanted to ask me if I had any suggestions for my replacement. The theatre program was enjoying great success. The previous year he had released the money for me to make a video that had helped recruit a group of very talented students. Denzel Washington and other former theatre students of mine, who had become successful, were interviewed on the video. So I was surprised when, after greeting each other, his first words to me were, "Dave, what happened to you?"

I told him how I had grown up as a Roman Catholic but had never known Jesus and never had had a relationship with Him. Many times I had gone to confession, but I always knew that I would turn around and sin again. I told him I no longer believed in the Roman Catholic religious sacramental system, such as the doctrine of transubstantiation, because it wasn't scriptural. I described how I had met Jesus and how I was baptized in water and in the Holy Spirit according to the Scriptures. I quoted Jesus' words in Acts 1:8 to him, "You shall receive power when the Holy Spirit has come upon you," and I explained how this power had set me free from alcohol addiction and lust for women. He had tears in his eyes. "I've never had any experiences like that," he said to me.

"You can," I encouraged him. I told him I was disappointed that there were New Age practices being taught by some of the priests and other faculty, and that the Word of God was mocked in the university's Old and New Testament classes I had attended. Then I asked him, "Do you believe that Jesus is the only way to salvation?"

There was a long pause. He measured his words. "Yes, I do," he replied.

"Then this university doesn't make any sense, because the truth is not taught here. And that's why I have to go."

I thanked him for all his support, then I gave him a copy of *The Cross and the Switchblade*. As I left, I remembered that a Fordham Jesuit had once come to David Wilkerson and asked about the baptism of the Holy Spirit, as recounted in Chapter Twenty-One of *The Cross and the Switchblade*. I hoped it would make an impact on him.

A reporter from the student newspaper interviewed me. She wrote a long article about my history at Fordham, and also about how I had met Jesus. My testimony was published for the entire campus to read. Several of my students came to my office crying and asked, "Why do you have to leave?" I told them I had to follow Jesus and that He was calling me to work for Him. Although some of my colleagues were warm and understanding, others I had known for years now avoided me and wouldn't ride in the same elevator with me.

Leaving the security of a tenured position in the university system was a big step for me. However the Lord had reassured me with this Scripture: "I will make peace your administrators" (Is. 60:17).

That June, in a packed Philharmonic Hall at Lincoln Center for the Performing Arts, wearing my Doctor of Philosophy cap and gown, I gave awards to my students for the last time. As the graduation ceremony finished, President O'Hare turned to me. In front of the faculty, students, parents, and guests, he said, "And we'll be praying for Dr. Davis as he begins his new work in Israel."

Times Square Church was bursting at the seams. We had outgrown the Nederlander and the Lord had told

David Wilkerson that He was going to give us the famous Mark Hellinger Theatre on 51st Street. The Hellinger is a registered New York City landmark, considered by many to be the most beautiful theatre in New York. We began to pray for the theatre as a congregation. At that time the most expensive musical in Broadway history, "Legs Diamond," was rehearsing in the Hellinger. If it was a success and had a long run, the church wouldn't get the theatre.

The play was an abomination. It championed homosexuality and took place in a brothel. A famous night club singer, who was making his Broadway debut, starred in the musical. We prayed for the people involved in the production, but we also prayed that the show would receive bad reviews in the newspapers and on television. We heard reports that there were all kinds of problems with the scenery. Several times the opening date was pushed back. Finally, on opening night, some people came out of the theatre at the intermission saying things like, "Fifty dollars for that garbage! What a rip-off!" The show received the worst reviews in Broadway history. It is now a legendary "flop." Afterward the star of the production said on a TV talk show, "God closed our show." He later died of AIDS.

The Mark Hellinger was put up for sale, and Times Square Church bought the theatre outright. One morning, I joined Brother Dave and Gwen, some of their friends and several other church workers at the Mark Hellinger. We entered the lobby of the theatre and surveyed the place. Spectacular, carved angels hovered overhead, ornate pillars supported the massive structure, and oil murals graced the walls and ceiling of the high rotunda. While we were entering the front door of the theatre, the union stage hands were on the stage, tearing down the scenery from "Legs Diamond" and throwing it out the back door.

The foreman asked Brother Dave if it would be all right to leave a piece of pink scenery standing just inside the ornate proscenium that framed the large stage. "No," he answered, "it all has to go." I watched as the garbage, like that of my old world, was broken into pieces and thrown out of God's house. In contrast, I noticed that high above the stage was a beautiful, golden, sculpted crown.

In March, as the church prepared to move from 41st Street to 51st Street, I returned to Israel for two weeks to "spy out the land." I wanted to ascertain the extent of the drug problem, and to seek the Lord about where and with whom I might begin to work. Pastor Wilkerson gave me his file on Israel. In it there were letters from two Arab pastors, from Bethlehem and Galilee, who had written to him as early as 1981, asking for help with the drug problem.

As I traveled throughout Israel, meeting with Jewish and Arab congregational leaders, everyone confirmed that there was indeed a drug epidemic in Israel and that it was getting worse. They all agreed that a ministry, such as I proposed, was needed.

The Syrian-controlled Beka'a valley in Lebanon was a major international supplier of opium and hashish. Syrian army trucks, helicopters, and naval ships were used routinely to transport the drugs through Syria, and to Syrian ports and places along the Turkish border. At that time, the US drug enforcement agency estimated that Syria's profit from these sales was about $1 billion annually. Lebanon was one of the world's cocaine capitals, and it was estimated that twenty percent of the heroin distributed in the United States also came from the Lebanon's Beka'a valley.

Huge quantities of drugs were also systematically smuggled into Israel across Israel's borders with Lebanon and Egypt, through the sea port of Haifa, and the international airport. The Israeli army and public school system were plagued by the problem. The government was attempting to keep the scope of the situation quiet as it tried to find a solution, but there was no doubt about it—drugs had infiltrated Israeli society.

In my travels I continued to gather more first-hand information. In Jerusalem's Old City drug abuse was particularly rampant. One social worker told me that there was a drug addict in every third home in the Muslim and Christian quarters of the Old City.

At Nazareth Hospital, which is run by evangelical believers, the doctor in charge of the emergency room told me about young Arabs who die from drug overdoses. There had been a recent drug-related murder on the main street of Nazareth, and people were afraid to go downtown after dark.

In the Galilee area, I became acquainted with two particular Arab leaders who were trying to help addicts as best they could. Later, I went to a meeting at the small Arab Baptist Church in Haifa and heard a young Arab named Josef preach against "sin in the camp." The Holy Spirit told me I would work with him one day.

As I waited to fly out of Ben Gurion Airport back to New York on March 15, 1989, I picked up the Jerusalem Post. "At least 40,000 Drug Dealers in Israel" a front-page headline screamed. The drug epidemic in Israel had gone public. One source in the article estimated 100,000 hard drug users in a nation of less than five million people and others even believed there were twice that many. A Knesset (Israeli Parliament) member said, "Addiction is the

Number Two problem in Israel after security." The article referred to the "drug plague" that had come upon the land. For me, this was the final confirmation of our call. When I returned to New York, I reported to David Wilkerson about what I had learned. He wasn't surprised.

For more than a year, I had been preparing to be ordained with World Challenge, the non-denominational, international ministers' fellowship founded by David Wilkerson. When I returned from Israel, I finished my studies and took the examination. I had been asking the Lord to show me and teach me what it really meant to be an ordained minister of His gospel. I received what I consider to be a life verse: "You did not choose Me, but I chose you, and appointed you, that you should go and bear fruit, and that your fruit should remain…" (Jn. 15:16).

On Sunday morning, April 9, 1989, I knelt on the stage of the Mark Hellinger Theatre. Years ago I had attended the Tony Awards here, wearing a tuxedo and drinking champagne. But now, holy men of God laid hands on me and prayed for me. I was broken inside, overwhelmed by the goodness of God. Only God could have written this drama.

As my time at Fordham drew to a close, I taught one last summer night school course. I had asked the Lord to give me an opportunity to tell my story, which was really His story, and to save somebody in the class. I showed the film *Equus*. When it ended I turned on the lights in the classroom. There were ten minutes left to my university career. A young man in the back row asked: "Dr. Davis, do you think the psychiatrist in the film found God?"

"No," I answered. "He didn't. It's the tragedy of modern man."

Then, to my surprise, he asked, "Have you found God?"

God had answered my prayer. I looked at the class and told them how I had met Jesus and how He had changed my life. A young lady in the front row started to cry. "Dr. Davis, I want Jesus," she said. We knelt on the floor of the classroom and I prayed with her. The students slowly filed out of the classroom, watching the scene being enacted at the front. Several lingered in the doorway as she poured out her heart. Later she attended Times Square Church.

Several days later, after marking my students' final exams, I submitted their grades and returned to my office. For a moment, I stood looking at my library of more than 1,500 books. Then I turned around, walked out, and left it all behind me.

In early July, Karen and I received a letter at the Times Square Church office from a believer friend in Jerusalem. Karen called me at home and read it to me. Our friend wrote to say that a couple in Jerusalem were leaving Israel for a year of ministry abroad, and that he thought their apartment was ideal for us. It was available August 1. I told Karen I would pray about it, and hung up. Jerusalem? I thought we were going to Old Jaffa where there were so many addicts. However, I'd never received a response from the brother who was supposed to be looking for an apartment for us. Also, we hadn't planned to move to Israel until September. *Well, there's nothing holding us here*, I thought. This was a month early. When I asked the Lord if this was really Him, this verse came to me, "Fill your horn with oil, and go" (1 Sam. 16:1b).

I called Karen, and told her I thought we should go. She said she had just shown the letter to David Wilkerson.

After reading the first few lines, he handed it back to her. "God's opening a door for you," he said. "Go."

In our last meeting at Times Square Church, Karen and I knelt on the platform as David Wilkerson and the other pastors prayed over us. I was shattered by the reality of God's mercy and my own unworthiness. The Holy Spirit came upon me with such power that I collapsed behind the pastors' chairs on the stage. A new anointing engulfed me and filled every part of my being.

Three days later Karen and I flew to Israel.

Chapter 7

Jerusalem

An Israeli brother in the Lord met us at Ben Gurion Airport in Tel Aviv. Gidon was an ex-drug addict who wanted to work with us. He drove us to Jerusalem and helped us carry our huge, over-stuffed suitcases up the steps to our fifth-floor apartment. The apartment, which we had rented for a year, was in the center of downtown Jerusalem on King George Street near the corner of Jaffa Road.

As soon as we had settled into our new home, we wanted to visit Frida and her family. I called them but received a shock. Frida's husband, Ibrahim, told me that Frida had died the previous week. The cancer had suddenly returned, and she was gone. We arranged to visit the family. This time, as we went through "the eye of the needle" to Frida's humble dwelling, there was no joyous reunion. Instead, we sat with a large group of somber Arabs who were visiting the family during the thirty-day mourning period. As we tried to comfort Ibrahim and Sabrina, I wondered why the Lord had taken this woman just as we moved to Israel. She was the instrument He had used to tell us of the drug problem. Our call had come from her lips. I didn't understand it. As the mourning period ended, Sabrina began to visit us in our new apartment. She taught Karen some of her mother's recipes, like "maklubi" and "majadarah." Some say that it was for "majadarah," a delicious lentil dish, that Esau sold his birthright.

Sabrina took me to an Arab Christian youth group, which she attended in the Old City. The Spirit of the Lord was moving powerfully there, and about fifty Arab young people had come to the Lord. The pastor, who was from Jordan, invited me to preach. I accepted, and I began to pray for a message to give these precious young people who lived in such difficult circumstances.

Shortly before we moved to Israel, Karen and I went to the original Teen Challenge Center in Brooklyn to visit a couple who lived and worked there. We wanted advice and prayer before we moved to Israel, where we hoped to establish the country's first residential drug rehab center based on the Teen Challenge model. We were blessed to see all the clean-cut, vibrant young men who had been transformed from a life of bondage to a life of freedom in Jesus. Abraham recommended that I re-read *The Cross and the Switchblade*.

As we settled into the Jerusalem apartment, I took Abraham's advice and re-read *The Cross and the Switchblade*. The day before I was to speak to the Arab youth group, I read a paragraph in David Wilkerson's book that changed my message and my approach to preaching the gospel in the years to come. In the book, David tells that he asked his grandfather for advice about his growing call to leave his pastorship in Pennsylvania and move to New York City to try to reach the gangs and drug addicts. His grandfather was a retired evangelist of English-Welsh-Dutch descent, whose family roots went back to the Protestant Reformation in Western Europe and the British Isles. Grandpop Wilkerson told his grandson that he had developed what he called "The Lamb Chop School" of preaching. He gave the analogy of a dog with an old bone in his mouth:

> "You don't grab the bone from him and tell him it's not good for him. He'll growl at you. It's the only thing he has. But you throw a big fat lamb chop down in front of him, and he's going to drop that bone and pick up the lamb chop, his tail wagging to beat the band. And you've got a friend. Instead of going around grabbing bones from people....I'm going to tell them about New Beginnings."[1]

I tore up the notes of the message I had been working on. The next day I walked into the Old City without any notes. I had only my Bible, and I intended to throw those kids a big fat lamb chop of love and hope and change. They met in a second-floor upper room, only yards from the traditional site of Jesus' crucifixion. The young Arab pastor translated for me as I spoke on Jesus' parable of "The Prodigal Son." I used my own testimony as an example and also spoke of drug addicts in New York whose lives had been transformed by the love of Jesus.

Just as I was about to give an altar call for these fifty Arab teenagers, a young man appeared in the back door of the room. He was blonde, wore shorts and sandals, and carried a backpack. He walked slowly down the aisle to-

---

1. David Wilkerson, *The Cross and the Switchblade* (New York: Jove Books, 1962, special ed. 1993), 36.

ward me and then stopped and looked at me. "I heard you through the window," he said. "You were talking about me."

Then he dropped to his knees, sobbing. He told me that he was a German tourist and had been running away from the Lord. After I prayed for him, many of the young Arabs came forward and dedicated their lives to Jesus. There were enough lamb chops for everyone.

We still didn't understand why the Lord had brought us to Jerusalem, but I took advantage of the time. For hours each day I studied the Bible and also read histories of Israel and Jerusalem. I wanted to know why this tiny nation, the size of New Jersey, continually dominated the world headlines. It was clear to me from the Scriptures that Jerusalem would be at the center of the coming storm, as the nations of the world would turn against Israel.

As I studied the Bible in Jerusalem, I realized that it was here in the Middle East where the Bible and history intersect. History was not the result of random, unpredictable forces, as the Greek philosophers or Tolstoy had thought. The events that had taken place in this nation, where I was now living, were not just a series of accidents, or simply the results of economic, political, or military forces. They had been strategically established by God Himself. My excitement and awe grew, as I recognized how privileged we were to be in Israel at this time, witnessing and participating in the events that Isaiah, Jeremiah, Ezekiel, and Jesus had predicted with utter accuracy centuries ago. God was in control here, and He had written history before it had even happened!

As never before I saw that the Bible is essentially a book written by Jews as an historical record of God's dealings with Israel, and it is intended to be an example to the whole world. In addition to that, I gained fresh insight into the Bible as a book of prophecy, and I came to the conclusion that the prophetic Word of God is the most powerful force in human affairs. God told Jeremiah that He was "watching over His Word to perform it." Here in Israel we were seeing the indisputable evidence that what God said He would do, He was doing it now. Our job was to ascertain His will and to align ourselves with it.

As I walked the streets of Jerusalem, the words of the prophets seemed to open up to me:

> "Proclaim, give praise, and say,
> 'O Lord, save Thy people,
> The remnant of Israel.
> 'Behold, I am bringing them from the north
>   country,
> And I will gather them from the remote parts
>   of the earth...
> A great company, they shall return here"
>   (Jer. 31:7b-8).

> "'Behold, days are coming,' declares the Lord,
> 'when I will make a new covenant with the
> house of Israel and with the house of Judah,
> not like the covenant which I made with their
> fathers in the day I took them by the hand
> to bring them out of the land of Egypt, My
> covenant which they broke, although I was
> a husband to them,' declares the Lord. 'But
> this is the covenant which I will make with
> the house of Israel after those days,' declares
> the Lord, 'I will put My law within them, and

on their heart I will write it; and I will be their God, and they shall be My people'" (Jer. 31: 31-33).

According to the prophetic Word of God, the Jewish people still have a divine appointment with their Messiah, a time when they will enter into His new covenant with them.

In our early months in Jerusalem, we also saw the condition of the body of Messiah in Israel firsthand. (The English word "Messiah" is derived from the Hebrew word *mashiach*, which means "Anointed One" or "Christ" in Greek.) We visited most of the congregations in the city and had fellowship with local Jews and Arabs and foreigners from the nations. Winds and waves of doctrines collided in Jerusalem. There was also a major battle over the Holy Spirit. For instance, *The Cross and the Switchblade* had been published in Hebrew by a Messianic publishing company. However, all references to the baptism in the Holy Spirit had been removed without the knowledge of the author, David Wilkerson.

Although our understanding of Hebrew was still quite minimal, we felt most at home at the Hebrew-speaking "Kehilat HaMashiach" (Congregation of the Messiah) in the Old City. The congregation was led by two brothers who had been raised as Orthodox Jews in New York. Some twenty years earlier, they both met Jesus and moved to Israel. Although their focus was "to the Jew first," they also had a genuine burden for the Arabs. They often preached on the call to purity of the Bride of Messiah.

Even though we were living in Jerusalem, I believed that God was going to plant the work for the drug addicts in the North. I had not forgotten how powerfully the Lord had spoken to me in Galilee and on Mount Carmel. Also, in New York the Lord had given me a very specific word, which I had recorded in my diary: "Go, tell His disciples, He is going before you into Galilee; there you will see Him" (see Mk. 16:7).

In a worship service at Times Square Church some months earlier, I had received a vision of a beautiful white, fleecy cloud covering that seemed to stretch from Mount Carmel on the Mediterranean, across the Galilee, and all the way to Mount Hermon on the Golan Heights. I asked the Lord what it was and He spoke to my spirit: "These are the prayers of the saints that have gone up for northern Israel for generations. I am looking for a remnant I can trust with My glory and then I am going to pour out My Spirit in northern Israel."

Later, I asked Him to give me a confirmation of the vision from His Word. I was learning the importance of being sensitive to the Holy Spirit, Who would always lead me to that particular portion of the Word that I needed at a specific time. This time He led me to Psalm 68:34-35 (NKJ):

> "Ascribe strength to God;
> His excellence is over Israel,
> And His strength is in the clouds.
> O God, You are more awesome than Your
>   holy places.
> The God of Israel is He who gives strength
>   and power to His people.
> Blessed be God!"

A couple of months after we arrived in Israel we received a call from an Arab pastor in Galilee. I had met him on my "spying out the land" trip about seven months earlier. He too had a burden for drug addicts and also had a ministry among Arabs in the prisons. He invited Karen and me to spend the weekend with him and his family. He also asked me to preach and Karen to sing in the Sunday meeting at their church.

We rented a car and drove to Galilee. As we turned off the highway and onto the road to the Muslim village where we were headed, I noticed that Karen was crying. I stopped the car. "What's wrong?" I asked.

"David, I don't feel anything for these people—my heart is so cold," she sobbed. "I came to Israel for the Jewish people, and now I'm going to sing in an Arab village in an Arab church. They've always been the enemy of my people. How can I go in there and sing about Jesus if I don't love them the way He does. I know God loves the Arab people, but He's going to have to do something in my heart!" We sat in the car and prayed.

Then Karen got out her Bible and read aloud these words of Jesus: "For if you love those who love you, what reward have you…And if you greet your brethren only, what do you do more than others? Do not even the tax collectors do so?" (Mt. 5:46-47 NKJ). Karen told the Lord how sorry she was and asked Him to give her His love for the Arab people.

I started the car again, and we drove into the village. I was so proud of my Jewish wife that day as she stood in that Arab church, singing, "Behold, I'm new in Jesus.

Old things are passed away and behold all things are new." Karen had received the Lord's heart for the Arab people.

I preached from Romans 4:17: "He calls into being that which does not exist." I said that I believed God was going to raise up a work for Arab and Jewish addicts, and I asked the congregation to pray for this. Afterward, as we sat with the pastor, he told Karen that a few years earlier, ultra-Orthodox Jews had burned down the meeting place of the Jewish believers in nearby Tiberias. He invited them to use his building for their Shabbat (Saturday) meetings. For a time the Jewish believers had worshiped in that Muslim village. The Lord again revealed His heart to us as we listened to this Arab pastor who had reached out to his Jewish brothers.

That November we held a conference focusing on the drug problem and its solution—the new life in Jesus. Don Wilkerson, David's brother, who had directed the first Teen Challenge Center in Brooklyn for twenty-five years, and Frank Reynolds, the retired director of the Teen Challenge farm in Pennsylvania, flew to Israel from the States. The two of them have probably worked with as many addicts as anyone in the world. About one hundred Arab, Jewish, and Gentile believers from all over Israel participated in the conference. During the conference the same Arab pastor and several other Arab believers from Galilee met with me and asked if I would start a work with them in the North. Don and Frank's teachings challenged everyone.

One night at the conference, I spoke about coffeehouse outreaches, and we all prayed for God to raise up one. As I finished, a young Jewish believer from Haifa approached me. She said she and several other young people were trying to start a coffeehouse ministry in the lobby of their meeting place in Haifa. She asked me if I could help them, and I said that I would.

Not long afterward, Karen and I were invited to minister in their youth meeting in Haifa on a Friday evening, and to the congregational Shabbat meeting the next morning. In the Shabbat meeting, Karen sang before I preached on Jesus' parable of "The Ten Virgins." I spoke about the five foolish virgins who ran out of oil for their lamps while they were waiting for the bridegroom to come. This congregation desperately needed the anointing of the Holy Spirit. Though it was not customary there, the pastor had given me permission to have an altar call. Perhaps half of the people came forward, and God touched many who were hungry for more of Him.

The Lord was opening more doors for ministry in northern Israel. Two days a week we studied Hebrew in Jerusalem and then commuted to Galilee each weekend. We met regularly with our Galilean Arab brothers at Nazareth Hospital to make plans for and pray about starting a drug center in the North. They had already formed a non-profit organization to work with addicts. I told them the Lord said that He was going before us into Galilee and we were to tell His disciples. We rejoiced and prayed and fellowshipped together. At the same time, Karen and I also helped to launch the coffeehouse with the young people in Haifa.

One night, when I was supposed to speak to the Haifa youth group, I asked the leaders if I could join them in their prayer time before the meeting. As we prayed, these young people opened their hearts and cried out in desperation to God to do something new in their meeting. The Holy Spirit fell on us and people began to confess their sins. The meeting never officially began. The Holy

Spirit was in control. At one point, I turned around and the room was full of people. I didn't know when they had arrived. Twice I tried to preach, but couldn't. People continued to cry and to repent. We started to sing, and another wave of repentance washed over us. Finally I preached and there was more conviction. Afterward, several young people came to us and poured out the troubles and sins that were on their hearts.

At Nazareth Hospital, I taught a two-day seminar on the biblical principles of dealing with drug addiction. Doctors, nurses, social workers, two pastors, and other interested people attended. Our group was a mixture of born-again believers, nominal Christians, and Muslims. When I finished, I offered free copies of *The Cross and the Switchblade* in Arabic to everyone. A Muslim nurse picked up a copy and asked me if she could use the principles I had taught, but substitute Mohammed for Jesus. I said, "No." I explained that the whole process was based on the knowledge of the Bible as the Word of God and of Jesus as the way to God. She thanked me and left the book on the table. I prayed that she would come back and get it. A few moments later, she came back into the room, smiled at me, and took the book with her.

I drove back and forth across Galilee. "Oh Lord, show me the house," I prayed again and again. "Show me the place. Remember Your promise to me in New York that You will build the house."

At this time the Holy Spirit gave me a word: "And Jesus returned to Galilee in the power of the Spirit; and news about Him spread through all the surrounding district" (Lk. 4:14). I had a growing anticipation that God was on the verge of launching a new work. However, I didn't know that our "honeymoon" in Israel was almost over, and the battle was about to begin.

Chapter 8

Mount Carmel

It was January 1990. Karen and I had been in Israel less than six months. One of the Arab pastors telephoned and said he and the other Arab believers thought they had found the house we needed for the drug rehabilitation center, on the very top of Mount Carmel. The house was situated on the outskirts of a Druze village, near the place where Elijah defeated the prophets of Baal. The Druze are an Arab religious community who live primarily in northern Israel, Lebanon, and Syria.

Karen and I met with the pastor and his co-worker, on the top of Carmel at Stella Carmel, a nearby Anglican retreat center. The view of the Galilee below was spectacular.

Together, we surveyed the large, two-story house that was available for rent at a very reasonable price. The building certainly seemed to meet most of our needs, with its large kitchen, meeting room, and eight bedrooms. Living nearby were Druze, Arab Christians, and a few Jewish families, so we thought we would fit in comfortably with our neighbors. We met with the owner to discuss the terms of the lease.

Our Arab friend said that it was important that we meet with the Druze mayor and explain to him what we planned to do. We made an appointment with the mayor and the following week I drove from Jerusalem to Stella Carmel again. The mayor did not meet with us for two days. In the Middle East, officials often like to prolong the wait so that they feel that they are in control. Intercessors we knew had been alerted and were praying in various parts of Israel for the Lord to soften the mayor's heart.

I spent the two days fasting and praying at Stella Carmel. As I prayed, the Holy Spirit led me to Ezekiel 34: 26,29, "And I will make them and the places around My hill a blessing. And I will cause showers to come down in their season; they will be showers of blessing...and I will establish for them a renowned planting place...." I was convinced that we were in the right place, and that God was going to move on and around the mountain. Then the Holy Spirit seemed to lead me even more specifically. The following words were powerfully impressed upon me:

> " 'Buy my field'...For thus says the Lord of hosts, the God of Israel, 'Houses and fields and vineyards shall again be bought in this land'...I prayed to the Lord, saying, 'Ah Lord God! Behold, Thou hast made the heavens and the earth by Thy great power and by Thine outstretched arm! Nothing is too difficult for Thee!' " (Jer. 32:8,15-17).

This word was as clear as anything I had ever received from the Lord; I knew He had told me to "buy a field." I assumed He meant to rent the house we were considering, which was about 150 yards from Stella Carmel.

Two days later we were ushered into the mayor's office. Pictures of the President and Prime Minister of Israel hung on the wall behind him. Most of the Druze are Israeli citizens who support the State. They serve in the Israeli army and are renowned as fierce warriors. Since they hold to the theory of reincarnation, believing that when one dies he or she immediately returns as another Druze person, death does not frighten them.

After drinking our customary cup of coffee, the pastor and his co-worker explained to him that we were planning to rent the house in his village in order to open a residential drug rehabilitation center. I told him that our methodology was to teach the principles of the Bible. "When a person surrenders his life to Jesus, he receives the Holy Spirit," I explained, "which is the power to set him free from drug addiction." I gave him *The Cross and the Switchblade* in Arabic.

The mayor was very interested and he seemed pleased with all we said. He said that he would send social workers to help us. I graciously declined his offer, but I told him I would be happy to visit the schools in his town and teach about drug prevention. He welcomed us to his village and said that the city would not charge us for electricity or water! We all shook hands and embraced.

The three of us drove back to Stella Carmel, rejoicing over the great favor we had received. That night we signed a contract with the owner to rent the building for two years. One of the men remarked, "A notable miracle has occurred for Arabs to agree so fast."

Karen and I still lived in Jerusalem and had six months remaining on our lease. The building we had rented on

Mount Carmel needed a lot of repairs. Regularly we took the bus to Tel Aviv to meet Gidon, the Jewish believer who had picked us up at the airport when we moved to Israel, and his wife Renee, who was to be our cook. Together we drove up the Mediterranean coast to Mount Carmel to work on the building. The four of us planned to move into the building together as the residential staff when the house was ready.

Josef, the young Arab man from Haifa whom the Lord had shown me the previous year, joined our team. We had the beginnings of a staff—two Arabs, a Jew and his Gentile wife, and Karen and myself. We had no idea how we would finance the project. World Challenge would help some, but as I prayed daily, I received a promise again and again that the Lord would provide for everything we needed—food, paint, salaries, and all our other quickly mounting needs. The situation became an adventure in prayer for us!

Exactly one year after I had submitted my resignation letter to the university in New York, I began to teach the Word of God to a handful of people. Bundled up in coats, huddled around a small electric heater, we sat on the floor of a very cold house on the top of Mount Carmel. We planned to launch the drug rehab ministry in the spring.

Karen and I were still struggling to learn Hebrew in Jerusalem and were commuting to Mount Carmel weekly. One day as I was praying on the roof of the building we had rented, I saw a beautiful rainbow. One end of it seemed to come right out of the roof of Stella Carmel, and it reached all the way across Galilee.

We were ministering occasionally at a congregation of Assembly of God workers and Arab believers in East Jerusalem. At a meeting in early February this prophecy was given to Karen and me:

> "He is teaching your hands to war, so that you may break a bow of steel. Many will want to join this work, but the Lord will purge and some won't remain. Those that I've called will stay. Take note of your wife. I have given her discernment to understand the workings of the enemy. Pay attention to her. You have been called to this work, and your fruit will remain."

They collected an offering of $500 for us. We were greatly encouraged. It was our first gift from the body of Messiah in Israel.

On the last Shabbat of February, six weeks after we had rented the building, about twenty Druze men walked up to the house. "We don't rehabilitate drug addicts; we shoot them!" they said to one brother in Arabic. "If you try to bring an addict in here, we'll shoot him. And we'll shoot the American and his wife if they try to move in here. Then we will blow up the building!"

There was no arguing with them. They were serious. They had weapons, and they meant what they said.

I called Don Wilkerson and told him what had happened. "What's a Druze?" he asked. I realized we were in a totally new and foreign situation and that our past resources, such as the Wilkersons, couldn't help us now. We would have to depend completely on the Lord and He wanted it that way.

When I recovered from the shock, I went to the Lord in prayer. Again and again I was impressed with the word, "Buy a field…Nothing is too difficult for Me." The Druze mayor, who had been so friendly, refused to see us or take our calls. We all met at Stella Carmel and prayed there with the British pastor and his wife who ran the retreat center.

Two weeks later, our Arab brothers called me in Jerusalem and said they believed we had made a mistake. They now thought that the building we had rented was the wrong place. When I hung up the phone Karen and I felt released. A spiritual heaviness, which had weighed on us, suddenly lifted and we felt an unusual peace.

Nonetheless, as the reality of what had happened sunk in, I wept before the Lord. "Didn't You tell me to buy a field? Didn't I hear Your voice?" I cried. There was no answer. He was testing us, to see if we would still trust Him. We were being threshed. "…Unless a grain of wheat falls into the earth and dies, it remains by itself alone; but if it dies, it bears much fruit" (Jn. 12:24). The vision had to die, but the dying was painful. We had gone from the mountaintop to the valley of humiliation.

Still I wouldn't give up. I returned to the house we had rented and climbed up to the roof to pray. Several Druze men gathered and started up the hill toward the house. I went down to meet them, but I couldn't even speak their language. I wanted to tell them Jesus loved them and had died for them. We just stood there. I felt helpless. Finally, I got in my car and drove away.

In the meantime, I continued to visit drug addicts in their homes in Haifa with Josef and another Arab pastor. A whole family—father, mother, daughter, and son (a heroin addict)—all knelt on the floor and wept as the father asked his son to forgive him. My pastor friend said he had never seen such a thing. "What happened in there?" he asked me as we left.

"The Holy Spirit came—that's what happened!" I replied.

The Lord was still leading me to addicts in Haifa at the foot of Mount Carmel, but we had lost the house on the top of the mountain. I was confused and couldn't understand what had happened.

When God is silent, He is often trying to show us what is in our hearts. Pressure and crisis tend to bring out our true motives. As I sought Him daily, I gradually began to see my pride. In my zeal to do something for Him, I had acted independently of Him. I had imagined that we would neatly open that house with five Jewish addicts and five Arab addicts as the first residents. I was planning programs like I had done at the university, and I had run ahead of the Lord. "For all who are being [continually] led by the Spirit of God, these are the sons of God" (Rom. 8: 14). I wanted to be a good son. My spirit was grieved, but more importantly, I knew I had grieved His Spirit. This trial had shown me the ugliness in my own heart and I wanted that ugliness rooted out. I didn't want to do "my own thing" anymore. I wanted to do "His thing."

During this time of sifting, I preached a message in the Arab Church in East Jerusalem about the three Hebrew boys who were thrown into the fiery furnace. "Singing in the Fire," I called it. In the midst of their trial, "One like the Son of God" was in the fire with them (see Dan. 3:25). While our faith was being tested and refined, we received this gracious promise from the Lord: "And after you have suffered for a little while, the God of all grace...will Himself perfect, confirm, strengthen and establish you" (1 Pet. 5:10).

It was clear to us that we would not be continuing with the two Arab Christian men with whom we had begun to work. We agreed with them to sublet the building to Haifa University students. Although we deeply loved these Arab believers, we realized that our visions were not the same. As I prepared to take one last, long drive to Nazareth, a friend who knew about the situation called and said he had a tape he thought I ought to hear. "Who's on the tape?" I asked.

"David Wilkerson," he replied.

"I'll pick it up on my way out of Jerusalem."

As Karen and I passed through Jericho driving up the Jordan valley, we turned on the tape. Brother Dave was preaching from First Samuel, Chapter 13, on "The Awful Sin of Pride." King Saul, because of his pride, did not wait for the prophet Samuel at Gilgal. He disobeyed God and took matters into his own hands. As I listened to my pastor's voice on the tape, I looked out the window of the car. We were actually passing Gilgal on our left, while my spiritual father was speaking to me through the tape player.

Brother Dave confessed that he himself had pressed God when Times Square Church first began. He had been impatient while they were renting Town Hall for services, and he had wanted the Lord to hurry up and give him the Broadway theatre He had promised. Brother Dave repented for pushing the circumstances in the flesh and now, standing before the whole congregation, he confessed his pride. Deep conviction came upon me as I heard his words.

Pastor Dave explained that the sin of pride had destroyed Saul. The king lost his anointing, and in the end, he committed suicide on Mount Gilboa. Afterward, the

Philistines nailed his decapitated body to a wall in Beth-shan. As Brother Dave told this part of the story, we were literally driving out of Beth-shan, with Mount Gilboa on our left. I couldn't take any more. I stopped the car on the side of the road. I confessed my pride to the Lord and to my wife. Pastor Dave's message confirmed what God had been showing me. I saw more clearly than ever before how terrible pride really is in the eyes of a holy God. I knew I had to release it all, to let go of the vision and let God have His way.

At the meeting in Nazareth, I told the men that we were not going to be able to continue working with them. I explained that where there are two visions, there will be division. It was a painful meeting, but necessary. The vision of the house on the mountaintop was dead. Karen and I were on our own again, but we knew we had done the right thing. What we didn't know was that the Lord had a surprise in store for us.

When we returned to Jerusalem, I fasted and prayed fervently. We had applied for citizenship but the process had stalled. On April 4, the day our tourist visas were to expire, I woke up early and began to read the Gospel of Mark. What struck me was the recurrence of the word, "immediately." "And immediately the Spirit impelled Him to go out into the wilderness." "And they immediately left the nets and followed Him." "And immediately He called them…" (Mk. 1:12, 18, 20). The word is used at least ten times in the first chapter. When Karen woke up I told her we needed to go back to the Ministry of the Interior and re-apply. "When?" she asked.

"Immediately," I said.

That morning we returned to the same office where we had been six months earlier. It was the day before all the government offices would close for a week to observe the Passover holiday. Since our last appointment, the Soviet Union had collapsed and the Russian Jews were finally coming home. The previously empty halls were now packed with Russian-speaking immigrants. When the clerk called our number, we were ushered into a room where a secretary began to type up our papers. Fifteen minutes later we were standing on Jaffa Road, citizens of Israel, swept in with the Russian wave.

Karen and I celebrated at the best steak house in Jerusalem. Handel's "Messiah" was playing through the restaurant sound system. Karen wept as she thought of how the Lord had drawn her to Himself all through her early years of study as she sang and played the great sacred works of Handel and Bach. She remembered times as a young girl when the beauty of the music so overwhelmed her she could barely sing her part. Now, listening again to the glorious praises of the Messiah of Israel, she recalled a promise the Lord had given her years before when she first met Him. He told her that one day she would live in the land of her inheritance and bring His love to her Jewish people.

In the midst of what looked like a crushing defeat on Mount Carmel, God had planted us in His land. Karen turned to me and said, "He must want us to stay."

– Chapter 9 –

"The Valley of Trouble is the Door of Hope"

On the northern tip of the slope of Mount Carmel, there are two large, old Arab-style buildings, the remnants of what was once a believers' community. The oldest of these two structures, which overlook the port city of Haifa, was built in 1900. British Christians ran a medical clinic there staffed by doctors, nurses, and volunteers who treated both Arabs and Jews alike. One doctor lived and labored there for fifty years. Some elderly inhabitants of Haifa still fondly remember Dr. Churcher making house calls on his donkey, and carrying his black bag and black Bible. The little stone building where he stabled his donkey is still standing.

Later in the 1930's, Hannah Hurnard, the author of *Hinds' Feet on High Places*, lived and worked on this same compound. In her book, *Wayfarer in the Land*, she relates how the Lord spoke to her in a prayer meeting at "the compound." He told her to visit every Jewish settlement in what was then called "Palestine."

(In A.D. 70, after the Romans destroyed the second Jewish temple in Jerusalem, they changed the name of Israel to "Palestine." Deriving the new name from the word "Philistine,"–Israel's ancient foe–the Romans attempted to eradicate every trace of the Jewish people. However, the New Testament is clear on the issue of the land of Israel. We read the name Israel in many places: Joseph, Mary, and the child Jesus returned to "the land of Israel" [Mt. 2: 20-21]; Jesus sent the twelve disciples to "the lost sheep of the house of Israel" [Mt. 10:6]; Jesus tells the disciples that they will not finish preaching in all "the cities of Israel" [Mt. 10:23].)

Hannah Hurnard asked the Lord for a vehicle and for a person who could interpret into Hebrew for her. He answered by sending her a Jewish believer, who was fluent in both Hebrew and English, and a car that was sent by her father from England. She obeyed the Lord and took the gospel to every Jewish town, and later to every Muslim village, often under very dangerous conditions.

On my "spying out the land" trip the previous year, I had been shown these two buildings and was told they were for sale. The organization in England that owned the buildings was having financial problems. Their local representative, a Jewish believer, asked me if I would be interested in buying the compound, but I had no leading from the Lord to start raising large sums of money. After Karen and I moved to Jerusalem and started to commute to Haifa, I occasionally spent the night in one of the two old buildings.

At the time when our work halted on the top of the mountain, the agent for the compound told me that an apartment on the top floor of one of the buildings would soon be available for rent. Karen and I went to look at it. The family living there told us that they and others had been praying for a long time that the building would be used to help drug addicts. We prayed with them that God's purposes for the compound would be fulfilled.

On the last day of May 1990, Karen and I were praying in our living room in Jerusalem when I had two visions. In one scene, missiles were hitting Israel and Jewish people were turning to a few believers and asking for New Testaments. In the second vision, Karen and I were praising God with others at the compound in Haifa. We rented the apartment we had been offered and moved to Haifa two weeks later.

Many believers in Jerusalem were praying for us as we moved North. Before leaving I preached a message to a congregation entitled, "The Valley of Achor is a Door of Hope" (see Hos. 2:15). Achor in Hebrew means "trouble." Though we had been in the "valley of trouble," we sensed that this move was a new beginning and that God was leading us to that door of hope.

Karen and I began to make our new home in the large apartment on the top floor of the Arab-style villa. Workers and volunteers from abroad lived below us in the apartments of the old three-story building. From our front porch, we had a view of Haifa Bay, the port, and the Mediterranean Sea. On a clear day, we could see all the way to Lebanon, which is about twenty-five miles to the north. I had a little study and prayer room where I could be alone with the Lord.

The compound, located on HaGefen ("the vine") Street, was built into the steep foot of Mount Carmel. Ancient olive trees, as well as fig, tangerine, almond, lemon, and even grapefruit trees grew on the property. The building itself badly needed renovation, and the once-beautiful grounds and gardens were now sorely untended and heavily overgrown with weeds. Since the buildings were up for sale, we were only given a six-month lease, through the end of 1990.

As new immigrants we were provided with five months of free, intensive, Hebrew language study. *Olim*, as we were called (Hebrew for "immigrant," from a root meaning "a burnt offering that goes up"), were also given a five-month stipend that almost paid our monthly rent. Karen and I walked to school, which was situated in an immigrant absorption center several blocks from where we lived. There was only one other American in our class of about thirty. All the other students were Russian-speakers from the former Soviet Union. I was probably the oldest member of the class and certainly the worst student. Just one year earlier, I had been a university professor, but now this doctor of philosophy sat in fear and trembling, panicked that the teacher would call on him and embarrass him again. This was even worse than trying to run the sound system in a Broadway theatre!

Of course, the Russians all wanted to know why in the world we left America where "money grew on trees," or so they thought. In our improving Hebrew, we were able to share our story and the gospel with many of these precious people. In the former Soviet Union, they had been severely repressed. Most of them had never owned or read a Bible. Even Russian books like *Dr. Zhivago* and works by Alexander Solzhenitsyn and others that I had read in the U.S. had been banned. Now, free at last in Israel, they were open to new ideas.

One morning, an Israeli Air Force Captain spoke to our class. On a large map, he pointed out how the Syrians and Egyptians had simultaneously attacked Israel at the beginning of the Yom Kippur War. He showed us how he had led his fighter group over the Golan Heights, where they had been confronted by Syrian MIG jet fighter planes. His best friend was shot down and killed.

Some of the Russian immigrants raised their hands. "Where did the Syrians get the MIGS?" one asked.

"From Russia," the Captain replied.

They were shocked to learn that the Soviet Union had armed the Arab nations. One of Karen's friends was very upset. "We never knew," she said to Karen after the class. She was very ashamed that her former government had armed the enemies of her people.

Each of us was required to give a five-minute speech in Hebrew. I was terrified when my turn came, but I asked the Lord to help me to give my testimony. As I recounted my past, I told the class that I had played Colonel Vershinin in Anton Chekkov's Russian classic, "The Three Sisters." Their Cold War attitude toward me thawed noticeably after that. Some of my Russian classmates began calling me "Colonel" or "Vershinin." Occasionally I even received a salute! As I was about to describe how I met the Lord in New York, the teacher was suddenly called out of the room. I knew the Lord was giving me an open door.

For her class presentation, Karen brought a little synthesizer and sang two worship songs in Hebrew. The school principal heard about her and invited her to sing for a *Kabbalat Shabbat* (welcoming of the Sabbath) celebration for the whole school. The day she sang we asked a group at the compound to pray for the gathering, while another believer and I prayed in the back of the hall. As Karen stood on the auditorium stage before several hun-

David with Anthony Hopkins during the filming of "Mayflower," 1978.

Karen and David at their wedding in New York, 1987.

House of Victory rehabilitation center, Mount Carmel.

Karen leads worship at Carmel Assembly Passover Seder, 1997.

House of Victory staff, Left to Right Ivan, Raul, Eric, Danny, Josef (1996).

View of the Galilee from the top of Carmel where we are building the new worship center.

David and Ron leaving House of Victory for King's Kids camp while "Eddie" says goodbye (Summer, 1994).

The Davis Family, Spring, 1997.

The Carmel Assembly worship center on the top of Mount Carmel. Over four hundred volunteers from more than thirty countries have worked on the building (September 1997).

dred immigrants and teachers, she read and sang the following words in Hebrew, from Isaiah 61:1-2a:

> "The Spirit of the Lord God is upon me,
> Because the Lord has anointed me
> To bring good news to the afflicted;
> He has sent me to bind up the brokenhearted,
> To proclaim liberty to captives,
> And freedom to prisoners;
> To proclaim the favorable year of the Lord."

The Holy Spirit filled the room. Some people began to cry. One woman ran to the wall and put her fingers in her ears. It happened to be our teacher's birthday that day and she came to Karen in tears. "Thank you so much for such a special birthday gift," she said. "It was so beautiful. It pierced my heart." As people filed out, Karen spoke to some of them about her faith and gave out several Russian Bibles.

Although we were greatly encouraged by the openness of the Russians, we were discouraged by the negative attitudes of some of the Jewish believers. When we were asked if we would be working with Jews or Arabs, we always answered, "With both."

People would say, "It won't work." Then they would look at us as if to say, "You'll learn." Of course our aborted attempt to plant a drug rehab ministry on top of Mount Carmel made it look like perhaps they were right. One Messianic Jewish doctor told me, "You can't help drug addicts. I know. I've tried."

"I don't believe in the wisdom of men," I replied. "I believe in the power of God."

Occasionally after meeting with some of these skeptical believers, Karen and I would go home and rebuke the spirit of discouragement. Then we would praise the Lord and continue to stand on His promises to us.

In contrast to the prevailing negativity, I was pleasantly surprised when four young couples asked me to start a weekly Bible study on "the walk of holiness," just one week after we moved to Haifa. One was an Arab couple, Josef and his wife, and the other three were Jewish couples. I had been praying that the Lord would show me Jews and Arabs whom He was calling to work with addicts and alcoholics. I agreed to start a Bible study on Thursday nights for these hungry young people, which I thought could also serve as a foundation for those who might want to work with addicts. I knew that if we hoped to have any success in ministering to people bound by the filth and degradation of an addicted lifestyle, our workers would have to be clean before the Lord.

Ten days after we moved into the compound, I was already teaching about the holiness of God and the believer's responsibility to walk on "the highway of holiness." I explained that the gospel of Jesus enables us to live a clean life in a dirty world. News of the Bible study spread. Within one month, there were fifty or more Jews, Arabs, and Gentiles crowding into our living room, kitchen, and hallways, and out onto the balcony.

Karen played her synthesizer and the high praises of God rang out over the compound in Hebrew, Arabic, and English. The Holy Spirit was beginning to move. We prayed for several drug addicts. Believers repented and confessed their sins, and a few couples asked for marriage counseling. Some people drove from other parts of Galilee and told me they came for "the Word and the worship." One year after we had moved to Israel, Karen and I were already trying to meet the needs of a growing home group.

Israel has an excellent inner- and inter-city bus system, but we knew we needed a car. Mid-summer, Middle Eastern heat can be torturous, and I often traveled to visit addicts in their homes. As we prayed about our situation, we received a promise from Psalm 121:

> "The Lord is your keeper;
> The Lord is your shade on your right hand.
> The sun will not smite you by day"
> (Ps. 121:5-6).

The next day a believer who was leaving Israel called us. He said he wanted us to have his car if we could just pay him enough money to cover the airfare to fly his family to the States. He himself was an ex-drug addict, and he said that he wanted us to have his almost new automobile to help in our work to reach drug addicts. We knew the car was a gift from God, and it was air-conditioned! The summers are so hot that most shops and businesses close in the afternoon. Many people stay indoors with the windows shuttered to keep out the heat. It arrived just in time for us to survive our first August in Haifa.

We continued to pray about the compound, which was still up for sale. Local real estate developers wanted to purchase it, knock down the buildings, and put up high-rise apartment houses. The New Age cult, Bahai, also wanted it. They were buying land and buildings all over the northern tip of Mount Carmel. Their international headquarters and golden-domed temple, which faces the tomb of their prophet in Acco across the Haifa Bay, are situated near us on Mount Carmel.

As prospective buyers showed up at our door wanting to measure our apartment, we entered into intense prayer warfare, proclaiming God's Word and calling on the Lord to "repel the onslaught at the gate" (Is. 28:6). Prayer went up throughout Israel and from prayer groups abroad to save the compound in Haifa for God's work and purposes. In the midst of the battle for the buildings, Karen received this word from the Lord:

> "...'I will cause the cities to be inhabited, and the waste places will be rebuilt. And the desolate land will be cultivated instead of being a desolation in the sight of everyone who passed by. And they will say, "This desolate land has become like the garden of Eden; and the waste, desolate, and ruined cities are fortified and inhabited." Then the nations that are left round about you will know that I, the Lord, have rebuilt the ruined places and planted that which was desolate; I, the Lord, have spoken and will do it'" (Ezek. 36:33-36).

During this time, two workers from a British Christian ministry attended one of our meetings, where they saw Jews and Arabs worshiping together. They had been ministering mainly in the Muslim world and had received the same "one new man" vision for Mount Carmel in their prayer meetings in Britain. Even before Karen and I moved to Israel, they had been praying for the compound and Stella Carmel, the retreat center at the top of the mountain. These two intercessors were staying with us when the leaders of a Swiss evangelical organization arrived at the compound.

The Swiss ministry had a long history of outreach to Jews and Arabs in Israel, and they owned a conference center for believers on Mount Carmel. As we met with the Swiss leadership team in our living room, our two new British friends prayed quietly in the guest room. I described the immensity of the drug plague in Haifa and all of Israel, and how we wanted to be a "Good Samaritan" ministry to Arabs and Jews. I shared what we believed was the Lord's vision for our work: to raise up a ministry to Jewish and Arab drug addicts and alcoholics based on Isaiah 58:7-8:

> "Is it not to divide your bread with the hungry,
> And bring the homeless poor into the house;
> When you see the naked, to cover him;
> And not to hide yourself from your own flesh?
> Then your light will break out like the dawn,
> And your recovery will speedily spring forth;
> And your righteousness will go before you;
> The glory of the Lord will be your rear guard."

As we stood on the porch looking toward the harbor, I asked the director where he was born. Assuming the answer would be Switzerland, Mr. Meyer surprised me when he answered, "Haifa." His father and grandfather had worked on Mount Carmel and in Galilee, sharing the gospel with Jews and Arabs. He had grown up in Haifa, and he even remembered riding up the mountain on a donkey when he was young. He pointed toward the central bus station. "My father is buried in the cemetery over there near the bus station," he said.

Mr. Meyer was obviously upset about what he had just heard concerning the drug epidemic in Haifa. I told him

I believed that we were called to continue the work of the pioneers who had gone before us in the medical clinic at the compound, ministering to the whole person–body, soul, and spirit. We all prayed together before they left.

In our meetings, we prayed more fervently than ever for the compound. All over the world believers were praying that these Swiss Christians would buy the buildings and not allow such an important outpost to fall into the hands of the enemies of the Kingdom of God. Three weeks later the phone rang and Karen answered it. At the end of the phone conversation she turned to me. "The Swiss have decided to buy the compound," she said. "They want us to start the rehab center here." We both knelt and thanked the Lord!

Near the conclusion of one Thursday night meeting in our apartment, the presence of the Lord was particularly sweet. The message that night had been about the danger of offering "strange incense" to Him (Ex. 30:9). He had chastened us by His Word and now, out of the silence of His presence, there arose a pure, spontaneous praise that filled the room. Karen led us as we sang praises in Arabic, Hebrew, and English. I was amazed as I looked around at our new family here: Jews, Arabs, workers from Australia, New Zealand, Sweden, Norway, Romania, Africa, Japan, Korea, Russia, England, Argentina. In our midst were a Holocaust survivor, an ex-Muslim who had been recently baptized in the Mediterranean Sea, and former members of an Arabic rock band who had left the world of night-clubs to serve Jesus. I was overwhelmed by the faithfulness of God as I prayed the words of King David: "Who am I, O Lord God, and what is my house, that Thou hast brought me this far?" (2 Sam. 7:18b).

As God continued to bless our Thursday night meetings, I also preached in various local churches, and occasionally at the Stella Carmel Retreat Center. In early September I was asked to give a message at a weekly meeting at Nazareth Hospital. I sensed that I was to speak from Romans 11, about God's purposes for the Jews. I knew it would be a very sensitive issue since Nazareth is now an Arab town with very strong Muslim and communist influences. Only Arabs and those working among them would be in the meeting. As I sat on the little porch outside of my study, praying about my dilemma, I read these words:

> "But if some of the branches [Jews] were broken off, and you, being a wild olive [Gentiles], were grafted in among them and became partaker with them of the rich root of the olive tree, do not be arrogant toward the branches; but if you are arrogant, remember that is not you who supports the root, but the root supports you....they were broken off for their unbelief, but you stand by your faith. Do not be conceited, but fear; for if God did not spare the natural branches, neither will He spare you" (Romans 11:17-21).

As I finished reading, I looked up and saw an ancient olive tree in front of me. Much to my surprise, a dead branch had broken off and was lying there on the ground. The previous day it had been part of the tree. I called Karen onto the porch and showed her the dead olive branch. I knew that God was telling me not to compromise in the teaching of His Word regarding the Jews.

Karen and I drove to Nazareth, and Josef came with us to translate into Arabic for me. Esther, a young Jewish believer who had been delivered of drug dependency came along also. In Nazareth hospital, I obeyed the Lord and preached on Romans 11. Some people were not happy. However, after the meeting an ex-Muslim, who had become a born-again believer, thanked me. He said he needed to know about God's love and purposes for the Jewish people, and that he had never heard such a message.

In the fall of 1990, the threat of war was in the air. The news media called it "The Gulf Crisis." Iraqi leader Saddam Hussein had already invaded Kuwait in August, and we knew he had missiles capable of hitting Israel. As Hussein and George Bush continued to "rattle their sabers" at each other, the Israel Defense Forces distributed gas masks to its citizens. We prayed a lot about the situation in our meetings.

Meanwhile, although the Swiss would not actually take ownership of the building until January, I began to teach several interested, local believers about working with addicts. We hoped that we would soon open a rehab center. An assortment of volunteer nurses and other workers from abroad still lived on the second floor below us, but the Holy Spirit continued to assure us that this was the place He had chosen to plant a ministry of rehabilitation and reconciliation. Again He spoke to us through His Word:

> "By wisdom a house is built,
> And by understanding it is established;
> And by knowledge the rooms are filled
> With all precious and pleasant riches"
> (Prov. 24:3-4).

We were confident that God was going to fill the house with afflicted and broken-hearted people–all those who are so precious to Him.

In late December, Karen and I returned to New York in order to pack up and ship all of our furniture and belongings to Haifa. David Wilkerson had also asked us to report to the church on Israel.

My message to Times Square Church was entitled, "The Gulf Crisis." I tried to describe what I saw happening in Israel and the Middle East. I explained to them that the real problem was the "gulf crisis" between the Jewish and Arab peoples and God. I spoke about Jesus' parable of the rich man and Lazarus, from Luke 16. The poor man, Lazarus, went to heaven, but the rich man was tormented in hell. In the parable, Abraham tells the rich man that there is "a great gulf fixed" between those in heaven and those in hell. The rich man begs Abraham to warn his brothers, but Abraham responds with these solemn words:

> "...'They have Moses and the Prophets; let them hear them.' But he [the rich man] said, 'No, Father Abraham, but if someone goes to them from the dead, they will repent!' But he [Abraham] said to him, 'If they do not listen to Moses and the Prophets, neither will they be persuaded if someone rises from the dead'" (Luke 16:29-31).

I told the people that we were trying to bridge the gulf between the people of Israel and God, before it is "fixed" for all eternity. The bridge over the abyss, the way across to eternal life, is Jesus. We who know Him have been given "the ministry of reconciliation" (2 Cor. 5:18). We are "...ambassadors for Christ, as though God were entreating through us; we beg you on behalf of Christ, be reconciled to God" (2 Cor. 5:20).

Times Square Church began to pray regularly about the Gulf Crisis. David Wilkerson even sent a letter to President Bush, asking him to call the nation to prayer. He quoted Abraham Lincoln, who had called America to prayer during the Civil War. The letter was published in *The Wall Street Journal, The Washington Post,* and *USA Today*, with this Word to the American people:

> "If My people who are called by My name will
> humble themselves, and pray and seek My face,
> and turn from their wicked ways, then I will
> hear from heaven, and will forgive their sin
> and heal their land" (2 Chron. 7:14 NKJ).

In the midst of the looming threat of war, we shipped everything we owned to Haifa by boat. As the deadline for Saddam Hussein to leave Kuwait approached, TWA canceled all flights to Israel, including ours. Only El Al continued to fly to Israel, and all their flights were completely full. The Israeli Army called up reservists, some of whom were in the United States, and many were trying to get home. We needed to be there, too, because it was our home.

We spoke with David Wilkerson about our problem. He asked if we were afraid. "A little bit," Karen replied.

He asked me if we had any disciples back in Israel. "Yes," I answered.

"You need to be there," he replied.

"We know we do." Then he prayed against fear and for the Lord to make a way where there seemed to be no way.

I went to the El Al office in Rockefeller Center. It was crowded and noisy. Finally, I spoke with a clerk at the reservation desk. She told me that all flights to Israel were completely booked. I asked her if she would please look again at her computer. She wouldn't. I prayed and then repeated my request. She was tense. "Okay, okay," she said. She looked at the computer screen, paused, and then looked surprised. "There are two seats on this evening's flight," she exclaimed.

"I'll take them," I almost shouted.

We landed in Tel Aviv two days before the Gulf War began.

Chapter 10

War on the Carmel

On January 17, 1991 at 1:32 a.m. Israeli time, the Allied forces, led by the United States, launched a massive air attack against Iraq. "Operation Desert Storm" roared into action hours after the United Nations deadline for an Iraqi withdrawal from Kuwait expired. As he promised, just two days later, Iraqi leader Saddam Hussein retaliated by firing Scud missiles at Israel. The first Scud missile hit Haifa at 2:30 in the morning on January 18 as we ran for our sealed bomb shelter. The following night we decided to sleep in the shelter. Another Scud hit Haifa at 7:15 the next morning. There was no missile attack during the third night, and in the morning a rainbow appeared over Haifa Bay.

In an attempt to keep Israel out of the war, the United States rushed Patriot missiles to Israel from West Germany. We watched Israeli and American soldiers slowly drive the missiles and launchers up Mount Carmel past the compound.

The Patriot missile launching sites were positioned just above us at Stella Maris, where the Lord had spoken to me through Archie Dennis' song on the radio in the summer of 1986. We now lived just down the hill from there. Two American soldiers told me that the Patriots were designed to hit airplanes, not other missiles. They had no idea if the missiles would even work. The first night they saw a Scud on their radar screen heading toward Haifa, they fired two Patriots. They watched as one of the Patriots just clipped the Scud and destroyed it. The American and Israeli soldiers jumped up and down and shouted, "It worked! It worked!"

On Friday, January 25, Karen and a friend from Holland went to talk to a Jewish addict and his girlfriend who lived on our block. As it began to get dark outside, I started to worry. Saddam Hussein surely knew that Orthodox Jews would be walking to the synagogues as the Sabbath began at sundown, and it would be a perfect time for him to attack Israel.

Karen and our friend returned at 5:45 p.m., and I told them of my uneasiness. We decided to eat dinner quickly and then go into the bomb shelter for the evening. Before we could finish eating, the air raid siren began to wail at 6:10 p.m. We raced out the back door and sprinted across the compound to the shelter. When we arrived, the door was locked and the key was not in the pre-arranged hiding place. We were locked out! As the sirens continued to scream, I yelled, "Put on your gas masks and pray!" We huddled together outside, crouching against the locked door of the shelter. Then the mountain began to shake. We saw two bright orange streaks shoot off from Mount Carmel as two Patriots roared into the sky. They raced up over Rambam Hospital where they met their mark with a tremendous explosion, illuminating the sky and the port.

Another Scud destroyed. Suddenly, the mountain shook again as two more Patriots thundered into the night. They turned and rocketed right over our heads to meet another in-coming Scud with a welcome, ear-splitting explosion. I prayed and cheered at the same time.

Later we learned that Saddam had fired seven missiles at Israel that Friday evening. An American soldier told me that his radar screen looked like "Star Wars" that night. On Sunday, I read in the newspaper that a family in Tel Aviv had lost the keys to their bomb shelter, so they went into a sealed room instead. Seconds later, a Scud hit the shelter head-on, totally destroying it. The writer concluded, "It's enough to turn an atheist into an agnostic."

In another incident, an elderly Jewish woman was found sitting under a table reading the Psalms. The roof and walls of her apartment were gone. We also heard of a Jewish believer in the army who was driving in a jeep near Beer Sheva and telling his Orthodox Jewish companion about Yeshua (Jesus). Just as the religious man began to curse the name, an errant Scud, evidently aimed at Israel's nuclear reactor, exploded in the desert near them. The man suddenly started screaming, "I'm sorry! I'm sorry! Forgive me!"

The morning after the attack, I shared in a congregation of Russian-speaking immigrants. The Lord had given us this promise from His Word: "Come, my people, enter into your rooms, and close your doors behind you; hide for a little while, until indignation runs its course" (Is. 26: 20). I told them that we don't need the keys to the bomb shelter if we have "the keys to the Kingdom," and we don't need a sealed room if we are sealed with the Holy Spirit.

As "Operation Desert Storm" continued, our evenings in the bomb shelter turned into nightly prayer meetings.

Our burden was for the safety of the Israeli people and their repentance toward God. Romans 1:18 became a living reality to me: "For the wrath of God is revealed from heaven against all ungodliness...."

We began to hear horror stories about Saddam's army raping, torturing, and butchering other Muslims in Kuwait. We prayed that the fear of God would come upon those Iraqi troops and that many would surrender. Since all religions other than Islam are illegal in Iraq, we prayed that Iraqis would meet believers among the Allied forces or in the underground Iraqi and Kuwaiti churches. We also prayed that many in the Allied army would call on the name of the Lord. We were thrilled to hear later about pockets of revival breaking out among Allied forces in the desert. After the war I read that 100,000 American troops were baptized in man-made pools in the Iraqi desert.

When Karen and I returned to Israel at the start of the war, we discovered that all the foreign volunteers who had been living in the building had left the country. To our surprise, we were now living alone in the large, run-down, old villa. "God used a war to empty out this house for His work," I told Karen. We began to hold meetings in the bomb shelter, and I continued to teach three, young Arab believers who were eager to work with addicts.

On my birthday, February 5, I fasted and prayed all day with these young men for finances to restore the building in order to launch the drug work. After they went home, I walked into our apartment. "Would you like to see your birthday present?" Karen asked. "It's on the kitchen table."

I picked up a fax from the table. It was from the Swiss organization who had purchased the compound. "With great joy we have agreed to support your work with this donation," they wrote. "We will declare it as help to build up the work amongst drug addicts in Haifa." They were sending $10,000 to help start the work. Karen and I could hardly contain our joy!

In the middle of the war, I showed a video of the Teen Challenge documentary, "Cry for Freedom." We wept as a spirit of intercession for the lost came upon us. Soon after, several of us visited addicts outside a nearby government methadone clinic. Six thousand Arab and Jewish addicts are registered there. Two Muslims asked Jesus into their hearts that day and some Jews received the New Testaments we offered them. A Muslim even asked us to start having meetings in his home. I continued to pray that the Lord would raise up, train, and support an indigenous staff of Arab and Jewish believers. We stood on this promise: "Thy people will volunteer freely in the day of Thy power; in holy array, from the womb of the dawn, Thy youth are to Thee as the dew" (Ps. 110:3).

I understood from the Lord that He wanted us to become a center of influence in occupied territory, moving in Pentecostal power. Earlier, when I told this to David Wilkerson, he laughed and said, "What you need is a Holy Ghost kibbutz."

The war in the Gulf continued but that didn't prevent us from preparing the land the Lord had given us. We weeded the gardens and planted radishes, lettuce, spinach, and onions. Early one morning in late February as the sun rose, I looked out of the window of my study and saw a tree bursting with white blossoms. The previous day it had been barren. It was fascinating. I'd never seen anything like it. Birds hopped on it, and fed all over it. When Josef arrived for our morning prayer meeting, I showed him the tree and asked what it was. "An almond tree," he said. "They are the first trees to blossom in Israel."

Later, in my study I read Jeremiah 1:11-12: "…'What do you see, Jeremiah?' And I said, 'I see a rod of an almond tree.' Then the Lord said to me, 'You have seen well, for I am watching over My Word to perform it.' " The word for "almond" and "watch over" are derived from the same Hebrew root. This tree is the harbinger of spring in Israel. It is referred to as "the watcher," or "waker," because it watches for an early opportunity to bloom. God was teaching Jeremiah that He was watchful and always on time to fulfill what He had promised. This truth formed the basis of Jeremiah's prophetic ministry.

No matter what negative words the people spoke to the prophet, Jeremiah knew that if God said it, He would do it. He was also teaching me that He was watching over His Word and His vision and that He would perform it in His time. I needed to trust His Word to me and be obedient to Him. As I looked out of my window at the almond tree, I was flooded with assurance that He was in control.

One crisp Shabbat morning as the war continued, I sat on our porch reading my spiritual diary. I read the entry about the dream I had had while in New York. In my dream David Wilkerson and I were eating from a wonderful buffet of food on the top of New York's tallest building. God asked me where I thought He wanted me to work. "New York," I replied.

"No," He answered. Then He turned my head to look at what seemed to be San Francisco Bay.

I read this and then raised my eyes. I was facing Haifa Bay, which many people say reminds them of San Francisco. The view from where I was sitting was the same camera angle I had seen in my dream. It was exactly what I had seen three years earlier. I was amazed and called Karen onto the porch to tell her what had just happened. "This time I know we're in the right place," I said.

An elderly Jewish believer, a Holocaust survivor, who had been a missionary in Africa, moved in with us for the duration of the war. On February 23, President Bush gave Saddam Hussein a 7:00 p.m. deadline to evacuate Kuwait or face a ground offensive. While eating dinner together, I laughingly suggested that Saddam would probably fire a missile at us at 7:01 p.m. At 6:50 p.m. the siren sounded and we ran to our sealed room. He was eleven minutes early.

The next day the Allied soldiers landed and the ground war began. On February 25, two harmless missiles were fired at Israel. The second and last one, was the thirty-ninth Scud. The following day, as the Allies approached the gates of Kuwait City, our furniture arrived through the gates of the compound. It had been in the Haifa port throughout the war. Three strong Russian immigrants carried our belongings up the steep climb to our third-floor apartment. Karen was thrilled when she saw her old upright piano being carried up the steps. We shared the gospel with the three furniture movers, thankful for every opportunity to speak of our Lord.

On February 28, I went to the post office to pick up our mail. Our monthly donations from America had increased sixfold. Later that day, a cease-fire was declared in the Gulf. It was Purim, the holiday when Jews read the book of Esther and celebrate their victory over wicked Haman who wanted to destroy them. All over the country, Israelis opened their sealed rooms and celebrated Purim and the end of the war.

That night, I shared this verse with our little flock: "He makes wars cease...Be still, and know that I am God" (Ps. 46:9-10a NKJ). In our meeting we began to pray and intercede for the survivors in Kuwait and Iraq. We prayed that the Lord would send an army of volunteer doctors, nurses, workers, and evangelists, who had a living faith in Jesus, to help the families of the victims. We beseeched "the Lord of the harvest" to thrust out an army of overcoming believers, not with weapons of man's warfare, but "[with] the word of truth, in the power of God; by the weapons of righteousness for the right hand and the left" (2 Cor. 6:7). We requested the Lord to send out some "trouble-makers" like Elijah—who would have the Word of God in one hand and the power of the Holy Spirit in the other, to help bring real peace and salvation to the Middle East.

The war ended, but I sensed it had been only a dress rehearsal for things to come. The body of Messiah was sobered for a season. I wondered how soon we would return to business as usual and if we had really learned the lessons of the war. I felt we were on probation and had been granted a gracious reprieve. "So He poured out on him the heat of His anger and the fierceness of battle; and it set him aflame all around, yet he did not recognize it; and it burned him, but he paid no attention" (Is. 42:25).

During the one hundred hours of the ground war, the Iraqis were prevented from using poisonous gas or nerve agents by heavy rains and turbulent winds in Kuwait. The experts said the winds were not blowing in their "usual pattern for this season." The commander for US Naval Forces in the Gulf said that Saddam would have used chemical weapons against advancing Allied forces if it had not been for "a change of wind that occurred shortly before the attack." The admiral said Saddam was blocked by "shifting winds."[1]

I wondered how many Israelis and Americans had seen the hand of God in the miraculous victory in the Gulf. In all the missile attacks on Israel, only one person was killed as a direct result of a missile, and twelve others died indirectly. The only casualty in Haifa was the young daughter of a famous Arab Israeli soccer player from Haifa, who suffocated in her gas mask. More than 1,600 families had been evacuated, and more than 4,000 buildings had been destroyed or damaged. During the war we slightly altered an old chorus that we often sang: "Some boast in "Patriots" [chariots] and some in forces [horses], but we will boast in the name of the Lord, our God" (see Ps. 20:7).

The Lord had "passed over" Israel, even as He continued to pack the country with Jews from Russia and Ethiopia. In one sense, the irrational attack on Israel had been an attempt to stop God's purposes by slowing down the *aliyah* (immigration), the return of the Jewish people to their biblical homeland. But His Word will not be thwarted. As I walked through the streets of Haifa, marveling at all the new immigrants, I remembered His Word:

> "I will say to the north, 'Give them up!' And to the south, 'Do not hold them back.' Bring My sons from afar, and My daughters from the ends of the earth, everyone who is called by My name, and whom I have created for My glory..." (Is. 43:6-7).

The Gulf War was over, but our war on drugs was just beginning.

---

1. Recent reports indicate that Saddam did indeed use biological agents against Allied troops during the time they were stationed in the Gulf. Just how widespread the effects are has yet to be determined.

– Chapter 11 –

House of Victory

Two weeks after the truce in the Gulf, we launched our drug rehab program. Our first two residents were a former Muslim communist and a Jewish immigrant from New York with a prison record. As Karen and I sat down to a communal meal with our "new family," I remembered the dream that I had had shortly after we were married. In the dream we were seated at a long table with young people all around. I had no idea it would include Arabs and Jews on Mount Carmel in Israel. Joining us at the table were Yusef, an Arab staff member, and Fabio, a Jewish immigrant from Argentina, with his wife Marilyn and their three children.

Late one night at the end of April, we received a forty-year-old Arab heroin addict named Ibrahim. Several believers went to pick him up in a town near Ben Gurion Airport. When they put Ibrahim into their van, the engine wouldn't start. Some drug dealers ran up to the van and tantalized Ibrahim with drugs in their hands. They pounded on the windows and shouted: "Don't go with them! You can't quit drugs!" Finally the van started, and they roared out of the village. Ibrahim sat there in the moonlight. He looked like a dead man, a walking skeleton. He had been addicted to heroin, cocaine, and *adulan*, Israeli methadone, for more than ten years. When he arrived, we took him into the bomb shelter, where a local pastor and I spent the night with him.

Ibrahim started to withdraw from drugs "cold turkey," which means without medication. Addicts who try to "kick" drugs go through withdrawal. They usually experience severe physical pains, migraine headaches, vomiting, nausea, sweating, and chills. Most addicts are terrified to go through this living hell that can last from three days to one week.

Other local believers stayed with Ibrahim around the clock, praying for him and reading the Bible to him in Arabic. Each time he complained of pain we prayed for him, and he said the pain left. He did not get out of bed for three days, except to go to the bathroom.

At our Thursday night meeting, three days after Ibrahim arrived, about fifty Jews and Arabs knelt and prayed for him while he was still in bed in the bomb shelter. At the same meeting a Jewish, drug-addicted prostitute asked for prayer. We brought her into the small apartment on the third floor, adjacent to ours, to live with a female volunteer who had worked with Teen Challenge in Holland. We also mobilized a "prayer chain" in which members of our community took turns praying for one hour each all night long. At 8:00 a.m. the next morning Ibrahim got out of bed. He took a shower, ate breakfast, and went jogging up the mountain! This was just one of the amazing "Mount Carmel miracles" that we began to witness.

Not long after this a young Jewish couple knocked on the door of our second-floor kitchen. Fabio opened the door. "Are you the people who help people?" a teenager asked. Surprised, Fabio invited the young man and his girlfriend into the kitchen for a cup of coffee.

Dana was five months pregnant. The parents of both teenagers had insisted that she have an abortion, but she didn't want to abort the baby. Dana and Yariv had no idea where to go or what to do, so they had been sleeping outside in a Haifa park. They were desperate. The two teenagers were also part of a New Age cult, and they had been "channeling" spirits with a Jewish guru. This guru encouraged Dana to have an abortion because, he said, the child would come back in another life. Since they had been taught by him to believe in reincarnation, suicide also seemed to be a reasonable option. They had a bag of drugs and had considered attempting to overdose.

I decided to let them stay in the house temporarily. We put Dana in our little upstairs apartment that we were now using for women, and Yariv slept downstairs. The next day we shared the gospel with them and then sent Yariv to a youth hostel, run by believers, in Eilat. On the long bus ride he began reading the New Testament in Hebrew that he had requested.

When we first moved to Israel, we were shocked by the degree of carnality and decadence that pervaded much of Israeli society. Haifa reminded me of Times Square in New York. Pornography is commonplace at newsstands and in video shops, and prostitution and drug abuse are widespread. Israel even has one of the highest abortion rates in the world.

One time, we saw hundreds of Jewish teenagers coming out of a local park in Central Carmel. Ear-splitting, rock-and-roll music blared over the entire residential area. The teenagers had been drinking and taking drugs. Some were openly smoking marijuana. The Israeli youth idolize and often emulate Western culture. Madonna and Michael Jackson concerts recently drew record crowds in the country. "Soft"-porn music videos from America, Britain, and Europe flood the TV screens. Sex, drugs, rock-and-roll, and New Age philosophies reign on Mount Carmel and around Israel.

As the house filled up with afflicted people, tensions arose among our staff. Our vision of a "one new man" community of Jews and Arabs within a family setting, which included men, women, and children, brought division. Cultures clashed. Some of our Arab brothers thought that we should work with male drug addicts only. They didn't understand why I permitted other types of afflicted people who were not addicts to live on the compound. I tried to explain that the vision included "whosoever" He sent and that the Lord's vision for this house was taken from Isaiah 58:7: "To divide our bread with the hungry, and bring the homeless poor into the house."

There was also sharp disagreement about the issue of smoking. These brothers felt we should allow limited cigarette smoking. However, I knew that in every successful, residential, drug rehab run by believers anywhere else in the world, smoking was forbidden. So we held to our biblical principles.

At a staff meeting, I reiterated what I believed the Lord's purpose was for the building as Jesus had said: "For I was hungry, and you gave Me something to eat; I was thirsty, and you gave Me drink; I was a stranger, and you invited Me in; naked, and you clothed Me; I was sick, and you visited Me; I was in prison, and you came to Me" (Mt. 25:35-36). It was clear to me that "a house divided against itself" could not stand. I read Amos 3:3 (NKJ): "Can two walk together, unless they are agreed?"

I realized that we were going to have to separate. It was very painful. Two of these young Arab men were like sons to me. I spent many hours walking on the beach, crying and praying for them. (Since then, we have all been reconciled. One of these young men rejoined our staff, and the other became a pastor. Karen and I recently ministered in his congregation.)

Two days later in our Thursday night meeting, six Russian immigrants accepted the Lord. Dana, the pregnant Jewish teenager who lived with us, also prayed to accept Yeshua as her Messiah. A short time later, her boyfriend returned from Eilat zealous for the Lord. He became our translator, and I had the privilege of marrying Yariv and Dana at Stella Carmel. The baby was born—a beautiful little girl named Ruth. They now have five children!

Yariv and Dana were representative of the epidemic we faced among young Israelis. The government figure for the number of drug "abusers" in Haifa alone is thirty thousand—almost ten percent of the city's population! Some of the best Israeli high schools in "nice neighborhoods" have been decimated by the drug plague. Fifteen-year-old Israeli girls have turned to prostitution to support their drug habits.

There are two, beautiful coastal towns in the North where the Zionist ideal appears to have worked. Swamp land, purchased from rich Arab sheiks, has been turned into beautiful cities. However, today, the residents are baffled and angered by the tidal wave of drugs that is overwhelming the new generation and by the corruption and crime that naturally follow in its wake. A perplexed mother of two teenage girls recently asked me, *"Ma la'asot?"* ("What to do?") Once I asked a policeman why so many people become addicts in jail. He threw up his hands and gave the same answer as that mother, "What can we do?" One prison near Haifa is even nicknamed "Little Columbia," because drugs are so prevalent there.

When heroin, cocaine, or LSD become the ruler of a young life, all ethics, morality, and inhibitions are swept away by the overpowering need for "more." One addict told me, "Pills are my god."

A side effect of the drug craze is the recent rise of "death metal" and "thrash" bands in Israel. Patterned after popular British and American groups like Black Sabbath, Megadeath, and Slayer, the two most popular Israeli groups, Incarnation and Leviticus, are made up of middle-class teenagers. Guitars blare and the members screech songs that mingle Christian symbolism with references to satanic worship, violence, death, and suicide. Some of these kids have been quoted as saying they would kill themselves if they weren't in bands doing satan's will. Satanic beach parties are "in," and the popular song *"Mashiach Lo Ba"* ("Messiah Is Not Coming") is the anthem of the youth movement. One band even uses Nazi symbolism.

A "thrash" music and paraphernalia dealer says his best customers for records, T-shirts, magazines, and newsletters are between the ages of ten and twenty-five. In the teen clubs in Jerusalem, Tel Aviv, and Haifa screaming kids bash into each other like bumper cars, and violence often erupts.

The lyrics of "thrash" and "death metal" are all in English because these kids long to escape from Israel to London or New York after the compulsory army duty that awaits them at age eighteen. (Boys serve for three years, while girls serve for two.) One "thrash" mother talked about her son. "From the lyrics, his vocabulary has increased amazingly," she said. "He can give twenty-six synonyms for bodily decay. He loves coming to the table and asking what the English word is for 'guts spilling out!' "

Organically linked to the counter-culture lifestyles of drugs and heavy metal is the so-called "New Age" movement. However, there's nothing "new" about it. Since the time of Moses, spiritism has been condemned in the Torah and the Prophets: "As for the person who turns to mediums and to spiritists, to play the harlot after them, I will also set My face against that person and will cut him off from among his people. You shall consecrate yourselves therefore and be holy, for I am the Lord your God" (Lev. 20:6-7). Consulting spirits led to Saul's demise (see 1 Sam. 28). Isaiah challenged the people this way: "And when they say to you, 'Consult the mediums and the spirits who whisper and mutter,' should not a people consult their God? Should they consult the dead on behalf of the living?" (Is. 8:19). Yet thousands of years later, self-proclaimed gurus roam the Carmel, peddling their lies and earning big money. Bright, curious, but empty Israeli young people, who are searching for meaning in the seeming insanity of the Middle East, are an easy prey for these spiritists.

Secular Jews are angry with the ultra-Orthodox Jewish community. Daily they hear on TV and read in the newspapers of the corruption, bribery, and hypocrisy of elected Orthodox political leaders who hold the balance of power in an unstable government. Several well-known Orthodox politicians have been indicted for illegally taking money for personal use. The youth are naturally turning elsewhere for answers and meaning.

The "New Age" openly and directly opposes the Judeo-Christian foundations of the Torah, which speak of a personal God and moral absolutes, as well as sin, judgment, and mercy through an atoning, sacrificial Messiah. In one instance during a meditation session, one young lady was suddenly reminded of a specific verse from Amos, which warns of judgment upon the children of Israel for turning to other gods. When she mentioned it to her guru, she was promptly told that it had come from a bad spirit and that she should never read that book again.

There are various branches of the "New Age" tree, but the poisonous roots all contain the insidious teachings that: 1) we are all gods; 2) you can raise your consciousness and become one with the universal spirit through a variety of techniques, many of which are adapted from Eastern religions; 3) we will all be reincarnated, which makes abortion and suicide acceptable options.

Yariv and Dana began to experience the authority and power of the name of Yeshua and the Holy Spirit over the spirits that had them bound. Their parents were astounded at the change in them. Faith in Yeshua is the door to freedom. The Holy Spirit is the operational power that releases repentant drug addicts and all who are bound in the death-grip of mind-controlling habits. He is the "anointing that breaks the yoke" (see Is. 10:27). He is the power of God who is released to "proclaim liberty to captives" and to "bind up the brokenhearted" (Is. 61:1). The key to deliverance is to receive a complete salvation that makes a person whole in body, mind, and spirit. Gradually, Yariv and Dana, as well as other new believers, began to live a new life based on sound biblical principles, led and governed by the Holy Spirit.

One time, we ministered in a house fellowship in Nahariya, a beautiful coastal city near the Lebanese border. Jewish immigrants, native Israelis, UN workers, and others, young and old alike, packed the house. An elderly, British gentleman prayed a glorious prayer to open the meeting, and immediately I knew I should get to know this man. Karen led in worship, and the Holy Spirit visited us intensely. My message was, "Is the King Your Friend?" based on Proverbs 22:11: "He who loves purity of heart and whose speech is gracious, the king is his friend." Ten Russian-speaking immigrants came forward and repented. Later, one Jewish mother called to say her son had become a believer in Yeshua that day. We talked with another woman whose husband was a rabbi. He had become a believer some years ago, and she had wanted to divorce him. Finally, she met Yeshua herself, after He appeared to her twice. She threw up her hands and said in Hebrew, "What could I do after that?"

I began to spend time with the British gentleman, Stanley Roberts. As an officer in the British Navy during the British Mandate days, Stanley had participated in the Battle of Haifa in the 1940's. He had been a pastor and evangelist in Britain before he returned to live in Israel with his wife Ethel many years prior to our meeting. He was an intercessor connected with a British group that prayed for Israel, and he held a weekly prayer meeting in his home. Stanley told me of the spiritual warfare that had taken place on Mount Carmel. He explained that there had been schools of false prophets on the mountain since the days of Elijah. He said he believed that Haifa was one of the most resistant places to the Holy Spirit in Israel, and that he knew "...our struggle is not against flesh and blood, but against the rulers, against the powers, against the world forces of this darkness, against the spiritual forces of wickedness in the heavenly places" (Eph. 6:12). Stanley was very supportive of our work, but he cautioned me that we were going up against spirits that had been entrenched here for centuries. As pioneers, we were on the front lines in the attack against the stronghold of drugs and alcohol, and Stanley warned us we were in for a war.

Several nights later, I was awakened at about 2:00 a.m. with the distinct impression that there were giants in the compound. I could discern two of them standing on each side of our building. They were ferocious and taller than the building. They had long mustaches, huge muscles, and bare chests with their arms crossed over them as if to say, "Don't try to move us, this is our place."

I woke Karen and described to her what I had just seen. Immediately, we slipped out of bed, knelt down, and prayed in the Spirit. We took authority over these spirits according to the Word of God, which states that Jesus defeated all demonic powers at the cross, and equipped those who believe in Him by giving us authority over all the power of the enemy (see Lk. 10:19). We proclaimed the power of the blood of Jesus. After an hour or more of intense prayer, the two giants left. We then felt released from the ominous oppression we had experienced in the compound for weeks.

Stanley Roberts preached in our meeting that week on "The Day of No Hope," referring to what Mary and Martha felt after their brother, Lazarus, had been dead for four days. The good news was that Jesus raised him from the dead. We were greatly encouraged, fed, and strengthened.

I wanted to name our new center "The Cave of Adullam," after the cave where the afflicted and wounded came to meet with King David. But since the Hebrew word for methadone is *adulan*, we were concerned that people might mistake us for another methadone clinic. Instead, the Lord gave Karen the name *Beit Nitzachon*, which means "House of Victory."

The victories, however, were few as we struggled to help addicts and others that first summer. The work was exhausting, and at times Karen and I would collapse into bed, utterly fatigued. Nevertheless, we witnessed the Lord's love and power touching Arabs, Jews, and an occasional Druze.

In mid-summer, the chaplain and the Christian Arab psychologist of Nazareth Hospital sent an addict named Elias to us. Elias was a handsome man in his thirties. After he smoked his last cigarette outside our gate, we gave him a shower and searched his clothes and suitcase for drugs. That night, I slept next to him in our bomb shelter. The Lord touched Elias, and he came through withdrawal without any pain. A few days later, we brought him into the main house.

That same night Karen and I were praying on our upstairs porch with a Christian woman from England for the "Lord of the harvest" to send us a single, male volunteer. We were understaffed and seriously worn out. Out of the darkness in the compound below, we heard a shout, "Does David Davis live here?" I wondered who was disturbing our prayer time and went to meet the stranger.

He was a tall, young American Messianic Jew from Times Square Church in New York. "I saw you guys at Times Square," he said. "I've been backpacking across Europe and just came in on a boat from Greece. Can you use a volunteer?" he asked. "I'd like to help out here, and I want you to disciple me. I'll do anything you want." We felt greatly relieved as our prayers were answered. Doug moved in with Elias, and the Lord continued to perform His Word to us: "Thy people will volunteer freely in the day of Thy power…" (Ps. 110:3).

We shared the gospel with Elias' parents and also with his Jewish girlfriend from Tel Aviv. However, after he had been with us for six weeks, he told me that his heart was "hard, like a stone" and that he had decided to leave. I pleaded with him, but he wouldn't listen. As he was leaving, I prayed with him and read him this warning: "For if after they have escaped the defilements of the world by the knowledge of the Lord and Savior Jesus Christ, they are again entangled in them and are overcome, the last state has become worse for them than the first" (2 Pet. 2:20).

We called his girlfriend and told her not to allow him into her house and not to give him any money, which he would surely use for drugs. A week later when we returned from our Shabbat meeting I heard these sad words, as I played back the messages on our answering machine: "David! David! Elias is dead! Elias is dead!" It was his girlfriend's voice. The second message was from Elias's brother in Nazareth: "David! Elias is dead! Elias is dead!" Against our advice, the girlfriend had taken him in and given him money. Elias had overdosed on drugs.

Doug and I went to Elias's funeral in Nazareth. There, an Arab pastor blamed his death on the Jewish girlfriend. After the service, I introduced Doug to the pastor, and explained that Doug was a Jewish believer in Jesus who had poured himself out for Elias the last six weeks of his life. On our way back to Haifa, I told Doug and the Lord that one day I wanted to return to Jesus' hometown with Arabs and Jews that He had set free from drugs. I wanted the residents there to see that, "Jesus Christ is the same yesterday, today and forever." Two years later, we would do just that.

– Chapter 12 –

Carmel Assembly

As we struggled to establish House of Victory, God continued to move in our weekly meetings. A number of people asked me to start a congregation and to be their pastor. I told them I had been sent to pioneer a work for addicts, not to pastor a congregation. Finally, as our Thursday meeting continued to grow, I asked the Lord if He wanted me to start a congregation. "I've already started it," I heard Him say. "Feed My sheep."

I called Don Wilkerson and told him what was happening. He said that he and his brother David were not surprised. "That's what happens when the pure Word is preached. Hungry people start coming," he said. "Go ahead!"

I had also consulted three leaders in the Haifa area. They all had sound advice, and encouraged me to pastor the new flock. The new Swiss owners of our building were favorable, too, and they reminded me that over the years there had been a history of meetings in the compound, some of which were even chronicled in books. I had come to believe that Haifa needed more than one new congregation.

At our Thursday night meeting at House of Victory, just one year after we moved to Haifa, I announced that the Lord had raised up a new congregation and that we would begin Shabbat meetings. We called our community *Kehilat HaCarmel*, "Carmel Assembly."

Initially, we met at the compound on Shabbat. However, three weeks later we received a call from the director of Stella Carmel. He invited us to hold our Shabbat meetings in the chapel there. The following week we met on the top of the mountain, back at Stella where so much had begun!

At our first meeting at Stella, we asked the Lord if we were in the right place. We wanted to know if Jewish people would feel comfortable there, or if the Anglican property was too "churchy." The next Shabbat, during our second meeting, a Jewish couple dropped into the retreat center for a cup of coffee and heard us singing upstairs in Hebrew. When told we were Messianic Jews who believed in Jesus, they asked if they could join us. They seemed to thoroughly enjoy themselves. They took the New Testament we gave them and agreed to read it. We had our answer. We had found a home right back on the top of Carmel, about 150 yards from the place where the work had come to an abrupt halt a year earlier.

I began to see the Lord's hand in planting the congregation on top of Mount Carmel. It is a wonderful, restful place for families to get away from the city, and for the children to play outside on the grounds. The previous year we had been humbled, tested, and pruned as we tried to start the drug work on the mountaintop. But now I realized that the Lord had used the episode to connect us with Stella Carmel. Then He gave us a better place for the rehab center down the mountain on HaGefen Street.

At the time, we had suspected that drug dealers were behind the threats against us and did not want us to draw attention to the drug scene there. Shortly after House of Victory opened, there was a $1 million heroin bust, involving a politician and his nephew in the village in which we had tried to start the work. A large cache of drugs was found in the forest near the house we had rented. Then, in the same village, a suspected addict killed a young Arab doctor with a butcher knife. I recalled the words of Jesus from Matthew 10:14-15: "And whoever does not receive you, nor heed your words, as you go out of that house or that city, shake off the dust of your feet. Truly I say to you, it will be more tolerable for the land of Sodom and Gomorrah in the day of judgment, than for that city."

I thoroughly believe in the New Testament model of plurality of leadership and I experienced firsthand the wisdom of this principle. We urgently needed help. Needy people showed up at our door at all hours. At one point, we were forced to remove our doorbell to get some sleep! We prayed earnestly the words from Ephesians 4:11 that the Lord would send or raise up apostles, prophets, evangelists, pastors, and teachers.

Karen and I were just getting to know Peter and Rita Tsukahira, a couple who had been attending our meetings. They were Americans who immigrated to Israel from Japan. In Japan, Peter had been an associate pastor as well as a businessman. Here in Israel, Peter continued his work in business, but like several other believing couples in Haifa, he and Rita had not found a congregational home or their place in the body of Messiah in Israel.

I asked Peter to teach at one of our meetings at House of Victory. We began to sense that he was an answer to our prayer for help. One year after our house group had begun, and several weeks after the congregation was officially born, I laid hands on Peter in our Shabbat meeting and installed him as a pastor. Rita helped to organize and teach our Shabbat school for the growing number of children in the congregation. The Tsukahiras quickly became instrumental in the foundation and development of Kehilat HaCarmel.

On Shabbat, people drove from different parts of Carmel and Galilee up to the secluded retreat center and the chapel was quickly filled. As Karen trained and led a small worship team, we started to experience a genuine release in praise and worship. Together, as a congregation, we also began to celebrate the biblical Jewish feasts, such as Succoth and Passover, which so beautifully reflect our salvation in the Messiah Yeshua. Arab believers, who had never been invited to participate in a Seder meal at Passover, now sat at festive tables next to their Jewish brothers and sisters as they began to understand the Jewish roots of their faith in Yeshua.

When a few couples left other congregations to join us, we were fiercely attacked. A letter, which contained false accusations and was addressed to David Wilkerson, was sent all over Israel and abroad to people who had no understanding of or interest in the situation. David

Wilkerson answered the author of the letter, saying how surprised he was to know that a letter addressed to him had been sent to so many other people who were not involved. Brother Dave urged this man to resolve the problem on the local level, but he refused.

The instigator of the letter, a pastor of one of the Haifa congregations, refused to meet with me. Several men went to him to serve as peacemakers, but he was still unwilling. When I heard he was leaving Israel six months before he was scheduled to leave, Karen and I went unannounced to see him. We told him we were sorry for anything that we might have said or done to hurt him. I prayed for him, but he would not pray with me.

Another congregational leader and his wife actually told us that they didn't want us in Haifa and suggested we go to another city. I responded by quoting the wise old rabbi Gamaliel: "If this plan or this work is of men, it will come to nothing; but if it is of God, you cannot overthrow it; lest you even be found to fight against God" (Acts 5: 38-39 NKJ). As painful as this was for Karen and me, once again we simply stood on the words of Jesus: "Blessed are you when men cast insults at you, and persecute you, and say all kinds of evil against you falsely, on account of Me. Rejoice, and be glad, for your reward in heaven is great, for so they persecuted the prophets who were before you" (Mt. 5:11-12). Right at that time we received a wall plaque from Mother Basilea Schlink, the founder of the Evangelical Sisters of Mary in Germany. It read:

> "Mightier than the thunder of many waters,
> mightier than the waves of the sea,
> The Lord on high is mighty!" (Psalm 93:4)
> "GOD IS ALWAYS GREATER
> THAN ALL OUR TROUBLE"

As the Lord was planting these two new works on Mount Carmel on the western side of the Galilee, He was establishing another new work on the eastern side in Tiberias on the Sea of Galilee. Claude, an Israeli evangelist from Tiberias, came to see me. He, himself, first heard the gospel on a radio broadcast from Lebanon while picking bananas on a kibbutz. He became a believer in Yeshua, and afterward, his wife and children also came to the Lord. Claude told me that each day after work he visited Russian-speaking immigrants. Whole families, he said, were accepting the Lord, and some were even falling on their knees.

Out of these home visits another new congregation was born, and Claude was quickly learning to be a pastor. He was also being attacked by other believers because of the new work. Not long after that, Pastor Claude brought about forty immigrants from his new congregation across the Galilee to meet with us. We welcomed our brothers and sisters into the overcrowded chapel and worshiped Yeshua in Hebrew, Russian, and English.

Carmel Assembly continued to grow. I began to teach the principles of discipleship through a series of weekly, foundational Bible studies on "Christ's Seven Letters to the Churches," "The Remnant," and "How the Master Trained the Twelve."

Karen and I were exhausted. That fall, we took a much needed, ten-day rest on the island of Cyprus. While we recovered, I asked the Lord to make me a pastor. I knew that I had much to learn and that the Lord wanted to do deep things in me if I was to pastor His people effectively.

Our burden for the afflicted expanded to include the unborn when a believer from the United States visited Haifa and shared about her work in the Pro-Life movement in St. Louis. We were inspired to begin a weekly prayer meeting about the abortion situation in Haifa.

One night, we showed our congregation a video of doctors and nurses who testified about how they had realized that they had been murdering children. Then we watched a six-minute video called "Hard Truth," which graphically shows parts of babies' bodies discarded in trash cans behind an abortion chamber in Houston, Texas. Tiny, dismembered heads, arms, and legs, and beautifully-formed little torsos silently cried out to us as the soundtrack, "Repentance," beckoned to our hearts.

Two teenage boys, who had been deserted by their parents and were now living at House of Victory, began to cry. One had just told me that he wished he had been aborted. A young woman read from Ezekiel 23:39: "For when they had slaughtered their children for their idols, they entered My sanctuary on the same day to profane it...." A spirit of travail fell on the group, and we wept over the horror of this sin in our land.

We began to see that exposing the true horror of the abortion epidemic might be a way to awaken an awareness in secular and religious Israelis to the reality of sin here in our nation. Centuries of anti-Semitism, at the hands of so-called "Christians," have given the Jewish people a collective sense of self-righteousness. Through horrifying events such as the Roman Catholic Inquisition in Spain, the Russian Orthodox pogroms, and the German Holocaust, the Jewish people have come to see themselves as the eternal victims. It is difficult for them to recognize the truth that "all have sinned and fall short of the glory of God" (Rom. 3:23). We hoped that if they had the opportunity to witness the destruction of babies, that they would begin to understand that they too are perpetrators, not just innocent victims, and that truly "the wages of sin is death." To that end, we applied for and received a permit to show videos and distribute anti-abortion literature in downtown Haifa.

Outreaches were organized. Hundreds of pieces of literature were distributed. We set up tables outside a large department store where we showed the videos. Many passersby were horrified at what they saw and eagerly signed our petitions to the government to change the abortion laws. One Orthodox Jewish man rebuked us. He said that it was wrong to view dead bodies.

"Is it wrong to view the dead bodies of the Holocaust?" one of our ladies responded. "This is another holocaust," she told him.

We joined *Be'ad Chaim*, the Israel Pro-Life organization, which opened an office in Haifa. Orit, an Israeli woman in our congregation, was appointed to run the office, and Peter was given pastoral oversight. Gradually, as Orit and others received phone calls and office visits, as well as went out to speak in schools and to other organizations, Israelis were being informed about the truth. Occasionally, a baby was saved. Thus, another new work, birthed in prayer through the burden of the Lord, had been planted on Carmel. A little more light was shining on that dark mountain.

Our meetings at Stella Carmel and House of Victory were packed to overflowing with Jews and Arabs, addicts and volunteers from the nations, all of whom were hungry for God. One Shabbat, there were six Jewish people who did not yet know their Messiah, Yeshua. The worship was so intense that an addict in the program ran out of the meeting. We were beginning to taste of the glory and wonder of God in our worship and new songs were coming forth. The room seemed to be washed in tears of repentance, joy, thanksgiving, and deliverance as people encountered Jesus, fell to their knees, and wept. Teenagers and children were also being touched. As I looked around the room, I saw transformed lives and grateful families growing in the Lord. I shared with our flock that we were entering a year of "breakthrough." After a season of planting and watering, a time for increase was approaching:

"I will surely assemble all of you, Jacob,
I will surely gather the remnant of Israel.
I will put them together like sheep in a fold;
Like a flock in the midst of its pasture
They will be noisy with men.
The breaker goes up before them;
They break out, pass through the gate,
   and go out by it.
So their king goes on before them,
And the Lord at their head" (Mic. 2:12-13).

More than one hundred people attended our meetings now. We had outgrown the chapel that had been built to accommodate only seventy. Some people had to sit outside on the verandah or in the hallway. We realized that we needed more space, so we started to look in downtown Haifa for a movie theatre that we could rent or buy. We began to pray that a particular large, pornographic movie theatre would close down and be available to rent. We also looked at two other closed theatres.

During this time, I traveled with other pastors from Israel to attend a leaders' conference in Cairo, Egypt. We met with a group of Egyptian pastors there and heard that revival had broken out in Egypt. Tens of thousands, primarily nominal Christians, had come to know the Lord. We prayed according to Isaiah 19:23-25 for the promised revival from Egypt through Israel, Lebanon, Turkey, Syria, and Iraq.

> "In that day there will be a highway from Egypt... Israel will be the third party with Egypt and Assyria, a blessing in the midst of the earth, whom the Lord of hosts has blessed, saying, 'Blessed is Egypt My people, and Assyria the work of My hands, and Israel My inheritance.'"

In Egypt, I saw the darkness and despair, poverty and hopelessness of a people in bondage to a false religious system. There, in what is considered to be a "moderate" Islamic state, spies infiltrated our meetings, and special police forces observed regular police on the streets of Cairo.

I visited "The City of the Dead," on the outskirts of Cairo. Close to one million people live there crammed together in shanties or in the ancient graveyards. Cairo dumps its refuse there, and many families feed off the garbage. The stench is overwhelming for miles around.

In the midst of this desert of darkness, I was privileged to visit and minister in a church, which was an oasis of light in a depressed, poverty-stricken area of Cairo. Several Muslims had come to know the Lord in that church—a decision for which they can easily lose their lives.

While I was in Egypt, I also met with the Field Director of the Israel Trust of the Anglican Church (ITAC), the British organization that owns Stella Carmel. He told me how blessed ITAC board members were to have a Messianic congregation that was reaching both Jews and Arabs meeting at Stella. Of course, he was disturbed when I told him we were thinking about leaving Stella Carmel. Then he asked me if we would consider staying there if they gave us a piece of their land on which we could build a worship center for our congregation. He said he didn't know how his board in London would respond to the idea, but we agreed to pray about it.

After I returned to Israel, our congregation moved from the upstairs chapel to the larger meeting room downstairs in order to meet our need for more space. However, we soon outgrew that room, too. Stella allowed us to cut two large arches in the wall between the salon and the cafeteria, almost doubling our meeting space on Shabbat. Every Saturday morning the Stella volunteers moved all the furniture out of the cafeteria so that our ushers could set up for the meeting.

Pastor Don Wilkerson came out to see what was happening on Mount Carmel and to ordain Peter as a minister with World Challenge. The retiring Field Director of ITAC, his replacement, and their wives, as well as the head of their Board in London, happened to be there at that meeting. Afterward, we all ate lunch together. "Would you consider staying if we gave you the land behind the retreat center?" the head of the ITAC Board asked me. "You could build your own worship center there." The land being discussed is literally the highest point on the Carmel range and is partly bedrock. It was only being used to burn rubbish. We discussed the proposal and then prayed together. Karen and I drove out of Stella Carmel with Pastor Don. "You know this is a miracle, don't you?" he asked me. "They are offering you the top of Mount Carmel!"

"I know," I replied.

"Do you have faith for half a million dollars?" he asked.

"Yes, I do." We prayed about it in the car.

The following Friday I received a call from Don Wilkerson, who had returned to New York. "I met with my brother David earlier today," Don said. "He asked me, 'Do you want to tell me what you saw in Haifa, or shall I tell you what the Holy Spirit told me while you were gone?' 'You go first,' I answered. 'The Holy Spirit told me to give David and Karen half a million dollars for whatever they're doing out there. Now, it's your turn.'"

Pastor Don told his brother about the offer to give us the land on the top of Mount Carmel and how we had agreed together in prayer for half a million dollars! David Wilkerson pledged the money to the project.

As Karen and I discussed this amazing turn of events, we saw the Lord's hand at work once again. I remembered what the Lord had said to me two years earlier, while I was fasting and praying at Stella Carmel concerning the building we were about to rent. "Buy a field," He had said. Now, we were literally being offered a vacant field at the very place where the Lord had spoken to me!

I began to study Jeremiah 32 again. The Lord instructed the prophet very specifically: "Buy for yourself the field with money, and call in witnesses...behold, I am the Lord, the God of all flesh; is anything too difficult for Me?" (Jer. 32:25-27).

Even though the prophet was in jail and Israel had been overrun by the enemy, God told Jeremiah to make a prophetic, public statement. He instructed him to purchase a piece of land as a sign that He would eventually gather His dispersed people back to the land and redeem them. The Scriptures could not have spoken more specifically to us and our situation: "For thus says the Lord of hosts, the God of Israel, 'Houses and fields and vineyards shall again be bought in this land'" (Jer. 32:15).

I called the committed members of the congregation together, and we discussed the proposal. Most were supportive of accepting the land and building our own meeting place. One or two were opposed to the idea.

In mid-October 1993, as we were in negotiations for the land, I preached a message entitled, "The Sound of Abundance of Rain," from First Kings 18:41 (NKJ). After Elijah called down fire from heaven on Mount Carmel and the Lord publicly defeated the false prophets of Baal, Elijah prayed. It had not rained for more than three years. Only this one man, who listened for the voice of God, was able to hear the sound of rain coming. Elijah's prayer was based on the promise God gave to him when the Lord had told him to confront Ahab and the king's compromised world (see 1 Kings 18:1).

My message called the people to prayer. It had not rained in Israel for nearly six months. Then at the end of the message, under the anointing of the Holy Spirit, I said, "It's going to rain today."

Later that afternoon, as we sat outside on the veranda at Stella Carmel with the ITAC representatives, the sky was clear. As we read over the proposed agreement that would give us the right to the piece of land, the sky darkened, the wind blew, and raindrops began to fall right on the documents. We all looked at each other in amazement and began to laugh. As the abundance of rain came, we moved indoors.

People in the congregation called one another on the phone. "It's raining on the top of the mountain!" they said. It took one full year of intense negotiations before the agreement was acceptable to both parties. The land was released, but the battle for the building had just begun.

Chapter 13

Drug Wars

On March 6, 1992, a quarter of a ton of heroin was confiscated in a $21 million heroin bust! Six Galilee gangs, in which Arabs and Jews worked together, were involved. In the spring of the same year, the Haifa University School of Social Work held a "study day" focusing on the growing drug epidemic in Israel. They reached the conclusion that drug use was spreading through all sectors of both Arab and Jewish society and was out of control.

We heard that Tel Aviv's two large methadone centers were overburdened and were swamped beyond capacity. Heroin addicts who couldn't get the synthetic drug were shooting up in the streets. Drug dealers had set up shops in the alleys behind Jaffa's methadone center. The government planned to open another center in Tel Aviv, two more in the South, and put a mobile unit on the roads in Western Galilee.

As the national "War on Drugs Authority" confronted the growing plague of drugs through secular means, the

Lord continued to touch individual lives. At House of Victory another Jewish addict came through withdrawal without pain after members of our congregation prayed all night for him two nights in a row. Some of these young Jewish and Arab addicts had the potential of being leaders in society. Instead they were outcasts.

One such addict, a tall, handsome Jewish man in his mid-thirties, had started taking drugs in the army. His once-thriving business was now failing. When he arrived at House of Victory his wife was threatening to divorce him. Karen tried to reach out to her with the gospel, but she was not interested. She was instead seeking answers in "New Age" practices.

One week after this man arrived, he said he had to leave because he felt a "stone crushing his heart."

"Let's pray that God will remove it and reveal to you that Yeshua is Who He says He is," I replied. As we prayed, he fell on his knees on our kitchen floor and began to weep. He asked for forgiveness from God for what he had done to his wife and children. He remained in my arms on the kitchen floor for some time. After awhile we got up and sat facing each other.

Finally he said, "It's gone–the stone is gone! I want to stay." As he was about to leave the kitchen, he turned back. "Amazing," he said with a pleasant bewilderment on his face. "I haven't cried in twenty years. Amazing." He went out shaking his head. He had been on hard drugs half of his life. A hard guy-but not too hard for God.

Later that Friday evening, at our communal *Erev Shabbat* (Sabbath eve) dinner, a worker from Germany and a young Russian played a Bach duet on guitar and violin to celebrate the birthday of our Swiss volunteer. Delivered addicts listened to the hauntingly beautiful music that filled our kitchen. When they finished playing I asked them the title of the piece. "Jesus, Joy of Man's Desiring," they replied. I was moved to be participating in this "one new man company" of Jews, Arabs, and Gentiles from the nations.

As word spread about the work, we began to receive calls from Arabs and Jews who were pleading for help for their drug problems. One desperate young lady, Grace, had been living a life of degradation and perversion. She had been beaten and slashed by drug dealers, and now her life was in danger. We brought her into the women's apartment. On the third night she was living with us, she was dramatically delivered from demonic oppression. Gradually, Grace's character started to change. The hard walls she had built around her heart over the years began to crumble, and a lovely, young lady emerged from behind all the masks she had worn. Grace was hungry for the Word of God. After she left House of Victory, she attended Bible school in another country.

An older Arab addict was brought to us from Cana. (This is the same village where Jesus performed His first miracle when He turned the water into wine at a wedding. Sadly, now, it is a Muslim stronghold.) His mother begged us to keep him at House of Victory. He completed withdrawal painlessly through the power of prayer. Arabs in Cana heard that Jesus still does miracles today and that His followers care for them.

One Jewish addict who came to us told me he had been doing drugs since he was twelve. He was mainlining (injecting drugs with a needle), taking a large quantity of assorted pills, and drinking a fifth of whisky daily. "You're taking enough stuff to kill an elephant," I told him. "Except for the grace of God you should be dead."

"I know," he replied. "If you won't take me, I'm not going to make it."

As I spent the first night with him, he was restless, prowling the room like a caged animal. He vomited once. Each time he got up, I prayed for him and he went back to bed. The second night he slept better, and in the morning he said he felt healed. He couldn't believe it. All his pain was gone. That night he handed over to us a small dagger he had been concealing in his belt.

Much of our struggle at House of Victory involved finding the right workers, who, at this time, were mainly foreign volunteers. A nineteen-year-old German became our much-needed gardener. He began to beautify the grounds and gardens, weeding them and planting grass and new flowers. On the surface, everything about him seemed wrong for working with Jewish addicts. He was too young, his name was "Christian," he was blonde and blue-eyed, and he spoke no Hebrew and only a little English. His heart was right though, and the addicts liked him. In his nine months with us, he transformed our grounds and was baptized in the Holy Spirit. He is now a youth pastor in Germany.

House of Victory also became an outreach center. We stocked one room with Bibles, Gospels, and tracts in Hebrew, Arabic, Russian, and Amharic (Ethiopian). We began to take the "good news" to the streets of Haifa. One night as we prayed before going out to a local park, I suggested to Christian that he stay back and pray, since he didn't speak Hebrew or hardly any English. But he said, "No, I want to go." That night in the park, as we sang in Hebrew and Russian, I noticed that Christian was speaking intensely in German with an elderly man. "I found a German Jew and told him about Jesus," he told me later.

From the front porch of House of Victory on Mount Carmel, Karen and I often watched ships from Odessa bring Jews from the former Soviet Union to the Haifa port. Before our eyes, God was fulfilling His word to gather His people back to Israel. However, we did not just watch the process from afar. We met and worked with these immigrants too.

The father of one family of Russian Jewish believers, told us how he had been imprisoned for trying to escape from the former Soviet Union. He was a rocket scientist, and now, here in Israel, he worked in a glass factory. His oldest son, Ivan, became the sound technician for our congregation and worked with us for a year at House of Victory before attending Haifa University.

In June of 1992, Karen and I returned to the States to take a much-needed rest and to report to the congregation at Times Square Church. We were blessed to stay at Hannah House, a new Times Square Church ministry for unwed, pregnant women, and widows. While there, God increased our burden for the abortion problem in Israel. All Israeli girls must serve in the army for two years after high school. Promiscuity is prevalent there. To "solve" the problem, the army offers the girls two or three free abortions while in the army. We felt that we needed to have a separate home for these afflicted women and others.

We drove to the Teen Challenge Training Center in central Pennsylvania in search of volunteers to help us in Israel. "The Farm" on "God's Mountain" had been established thirty years ago as a necessary "second stage" to the rehab work the Lord had begun in New York. It is chronicled in the book and film, *The Cross and the Switchblade.* Over the years, thousands of addicts have had their hopeless lives transformed. Eighty-six percent of the graduates of Teen Challenge have remained drug-free for more than seven years after completing the program (National Institute of Drug Abuse Statistics, from a U.S. government study).

The next morning we walked into the chapel. Two hundred fifty ex-addicts of all races were singing and praising Jesus. I spoke about the drug war in Israel and said we needed several volunteers for our work. I told them God was looking for "Timothys," who had the same heart and vision that we did. I used the example of Paul who wrote from prison to his beloved congregation in Philippi that he wanted to send his spiritual son to them: "For I have no one else of kindred spirit who will genuinely be concerned for your welfare" (Phil. 2:20). As a theatre director I had auditioned and interviewed hundreds of actors but this was no audition. That morning, I interviewed thirty graduating ex-drug addicts who were interested in working with us. I asked each one about his new life and listened to each miracle story of God's redeeming love and grace.

One Saturday afternoon, I preached at the Upper Room in Times Square where I had first worked with addicts. The Lord was still pouring out His Spirit there, and it was a tremendous blessing to get back in touch with my spiritual roots. I told the director that I was still looking for volunteers for Israel and so he introduced me to Eric Benson. Eric, a graduate of Zion Bible Institute in Rhode

Island, worked at the Upper Room. Eric told me of his burden for Israel. Because of his love for Israel, the other students in Bible school used to call him "Rabbi Benson"! Twice he had worked in Israel on a kibbutz, but because he wasn't Jewish he never felt fully accepted by the Messianic Jewish congregations there. When he heard me speak of the "one new man" vision for Jews and Arabs living and working together on Mount Carmel, he sensed that he was to be part of it.

The leadership at Times Square Church, Karen, and I confirmed Eric's call to Israel, and he soon joined us in our work in Haifa. Eric lived with the students at House of Victory for more than a year, serving and teaching them. The Lord was answering our prayers for a more permanent staff.

The Lord continued to touch hurting people at House of Victory. One young Arab addict from Haifa came through withdrawal without any pain. One day, I saw him pounding his knees with his fists and asked him what he was doing. "I want the pain to start, so I can get it over with," he said. It never did.

Not only addicts and alcoholics, but also their families and friends saw changes in their lives. This young man's mother came to a meeting and saw the change in her son. "He used to steal from me," she told me. "Now he prays for me."

This same man's lovely sister Sophia also began to come to meetings. She gave her life to the Lord and grew in her love for Jesus. Then Sophia met Eric, and they fell in love. Later, I performed their marriage ceremony at Stella Carmel. It was a joyous wedding celebration attended by Jews and Arabs, and the gospel went forth in Arabic, Hebrew, and English. We called it "the dance of the two camps." Eric and Sophia now live in an apartment on the top floor of House of Victory, where Eric is the assistant director. They recently had their first child, Sharon Rose.

Although the Lord had been faithful to send excellent foreign workers, it was increasingly difficult to maintain a residential program with volunteers from abroad, who sometimes stayed only for three months. We desperately needed a permanent, indigenous staff.

Delivered drug addicts and alcoholics need a substantial time of rehabilitation. They need to learn to live a disciplined lifestyle if there is to be any hope for them to function in society. The duration of most successful drug rehab programs is a minimum of one year; some are two years. We had no second stage of training, and so we tried to disciple the men in the confined environment of one large building.

However, the Lord already knew our needs. Karen and I were invited to minister in Finland in the Pentecostal Churches. We participated in their annual denominational conference. We also ministered in a basketball stadium and in twenty other church meetings all over Finland. The Finnish believers have a great burden for Israel. Even though there is a twenty percent unemployment rate, many Finns are very generous. Some travel into Russia to take clothes, blankets, and Bibles, especially to Russian Jews. We made many precious friendships there.

While we were in Finland, we had lunch with a photo journalist friend of ours, who represents the Finnish evangelical organization, Patmos International. They publish David Wilkerson's books and newsletters in Finnish, and they support works in Russia, Africa, and the Middle East. They had already made a very generous pledge to support the work at House of Victory. Our friend, Pirkko, asked us what we needed most. I said we needed another full-time, Israeli staff member. She asked if I had anyone in mind. "Yes, his name is Daniel Sayag," I answered.

Danny is a young Israeli who met the Lord in the army while reading Isaiah 53. He and his American wife, LuAnne, were one of the couples who had asked me to start the Bible study on holiness in 1990, which led to the birth of Carmel Assembly. He was now a deacon in our congregation, and LuAnne, who had been a licensed teacher in the United States, taught in our Shabbat school and was a singer on the worship team. Danny worked as a supervisor at Galtronics, a Motorola antenna company that is owned and run by believers in Tiberias and Haifa. I told Pirkko that he had a call to the ministry. She said she would discuss the idea of supporting him with the other Patmos leaders.

The next day, just before leaving for a conference in Washington D.C., Pirkko called us. She said Patmos had decided to support Danny with a full-time salary that would start immediately, with one month retroactive.

When we returned to Israel, Karen and I went to see Danny, LuAnne, and their two daughters in their tiny apartment. I asked him how long he thought he would be working at Galtronics. He said he had sensed that he wouldn't be there much longer. LuAnne confirmed that she believed her husband would one day be in ministry. One month later Danny joined the staff at House of Victory. The Lord had spoken to me about him from Isaiah 58:12 (NKJ): "Those from among you shall build the old waste places; you shall raise up the foundations of many generations." The Lord had provided the workers, and we all anticipated His blessing.

The house quickly filled up with a group of eight Arabs and Jews. For six months I taught them the Book of Acts, while Eric and Danny taught other Bible studies. The men grew in the Lord as the roots of their faith dug deeper.

Another man named Elias arrived. He had grown up as an orphan in Ramallah, an Arab town in Judea, the so-called West Bank, just north of Jerusalem. As a boy, he lived with German believers in the center of Israel before moving to Haifa. There, he discovered that his mother had been Jewish.

Without knowing Him, Elias experienced the mercy of God during his service in the Israeli army. While serving in Lebanon, three soldiers he was with were killed by a grenade, but Elias was unhurt. Another time, a terrorist stabbed Elias as he stood in his uniform at a bus stop in Gaza. The large, ugly scar just below his heart is proof of God's grace. However, after his army service, Elias became addicted to drugs.

Jesus set Elias free at House of Victory. His wife also gave her life to the Lord and was baptized in water. One night at House of Victory, they renewed their marriage vows.

There are many victory stories, all testimonies to the power of God's love and grace. Daniel was forty-eight years old when he came to us and had been an alcoholic for thirty years. He was seventy percent blind, so he listened to the Bible in Hebrew on cassette tapes. Daniel was emaciated when he first arrived. Later, he told me he had only intended to stay for fifteen minutes. He stayed for a year. When he first returned to Tel Aviv, many of his former friends did not recognize him. Now Daniel has an outreach ministry with a congregation in Tel Aviv. He sends alcoholics and addicts to us and sometimes returns to serve at House of Victory.

A forty-eight-year-old Haifa Arab with six children and six grandchildren joined us. He had been an addict for twenty-eight years, but he finished the program successfully. He gives me a gift now whenever I see him. The last time it was a bottle of newly pressed olive oil.

Raja lived in the Old City of Jerusalem, not far from Frida's house where I first heard of the drug problem in Israel. He was thirty-one, married, and had six children when he came to House of Victory. At times, he had stolen his children's milk money to buy drugs, and he was known in the Old City as a dangerous, hard-core addict. The first night that he was with us, I noticed that he was crying during our worship time. I asked Raja if he was afraid of going through withdrawal. "No," he said. "But I've never spent a night in a house with Jews before." I put him in a room with a Jewish ex-addict who had been with us for several months. Later, Raja told me he wanted to jump out the window that night, but the Jewish brother told him that he loved him because of Jesus and prayed for him.

Raja loved the Scriptures and was hungry for the Word of God. He spent one year in our program and then attended Bible school. Now he works with Dutch believers in the Old City, reaching out to other addicts. At times he also refers addicts to us. One day, after a group from House of Victory visited Raja, some of the neighbors wanted to know who those Jews were who were speaking in Hebrew. "They are my brothers," Raja told them.

Ibrahim is another Arab from the Old City who was in our program. He told us about "Force 17," a new, special police unit of the PA (Palestinian Authority). These Palestinian policemen had recently instituted a "reign of terror" in the Old City of Jerusalem. These PA police have threatened to break the legs of and maim drug addicts. They also routinely take them from the Old City to a detention center in Jericho. Two years ago, Israeli police discovered that addicts were being tortured in Jericho. Now this is Palestinian territory.

There is now a core of delivered, born-again, ex-drug addicts who have started a construction company in the Old City of Jerusalem. Recently, as they have been openly sharing the gospel, these ex-addicts have come under pressure and have been threatened by one of the ancient churches and by the Palestinian Authority. They were falsely accused and brought before Israeli officials. But the Israeli police dismissed them, saying, "For twenty years we have been trying to help drug addicts. These men are clean!"

Another addict who found Jesus was Danny. He was a thirty-one-year-old Jewish man, married, with two children. He had been addicted for ten years when he joined us. As Danny finished our program he said: "I was an outstanding criminal; now I want to be an outstanding man of God." He is now a home group leader in a congregation in Tel Aviv. Recently, his younger brother died of a drug overdose. Gonen had also been at House of Victory, but he left before completing the program. Standing at his brother's grave, Danny shared the gospel and warned the House of Victory students who had come to the funeral that they must continue to follow Yeshua.

As the ministry at House of Victory became established in Haifa, the Lord also gave us a burden in prayer for Jaffa. The old city of Jaffa, near Tel Aviv, is another drug stronghold in the country. It is overrun with Arab and Jewish drug addicts. However, there is also a Messianic congregation there. The pastor of *Beit Immanuel* is an ex-drug addict himself and has a burden to reach Jews and Arabs. We took a team to Jaffa to pray with him and had a strong sense that the Lord had a building in Old Jaffa that could be used for outreach.

A dozen of us prayed and witnessed as we walked the streets of old Jaffa. At one point, we asked a merchant if he knew who owned a little storefront shop that was closed up. We were shocked to discover that the owner was a member of the *Beit Immanuel* congregation! We laid hands on the closed up shop and prayed that it would be released as an outreach center to reach addicts. Immediately afterward, we met two drug addicts in front of the shop and prayed for them.

The little storefront is located in the entrance (or gate) to Old Jaffa. It was rented, renovated, and named *Sha'ar Nitzachon*, or "Gate of Victory" in English. Weekly, we sent a small team to witness to addicts in Jaffa. A number of addicts have come to House of Victory through this ministry.

Back in Haifa, we knew we needed to expand our facilities to provide a better place for women in distress. In an attempt to meet this growing need, our women's counselor, Tanneken, rented an apartment with another lady from South Africa, Renee. "House of Hope," a sister ministry to House of Victory was born.

The Lord began to bring afflicted women to live with Tanneken and Renee. In the first year, they ministered to prostitutes, battered wives, drug addicts, and abuse victims. Their problems ranged from emotional disturbances to eating disorders such as anorexia and bulimia, to suicidal tendencies. We are praying for more workers and believe that it is the Lord's desire to expand this work.

In the spring of 1994, we heard that a brother in Kiryat Shmonah wanted to do outreach there. We began to pray for him and about the drug problem in the town. Kiryat Shmonah is less than ten miles from Lebanon where bags of drugs are routinely thrown over the fence into Israel at the Lebanese border. Two days after we began praying for the town, I received a call from Tony, a Jewish believer who led a house group there. He said that he had found two brothers, aged 11 and 13, who were in trouble. Their father was an alcoholic, and their mother had had a long history of mental illness and had been hospitalized.

The boys were wandering the streets and not going to school regularly. Daily, their father would drink until he passed out. Then the boys would come home late and watch TV all night. At the time of Tony's call, there was no electricity in their house, and mice and rats prowled the abode. The government wanted to put the boys on a kibbutz, but they refused to go. I told Tony that House of Victory might not be the best place for two young boys because only older men who were coming off drugs and alcohol lived there with the staff. However, I agreed to pray about it and to talk with them.

Tony drove the boys to Haifa, and I met with them

outside on the grounds of House of Victory. Yeshurun (Ron) and David were both born in Israel. Their parents were Americans who had moved to Israel years ago, so both boys spoke fluent English as well as Hebrew. I explained to them that we were a residential home for drug addicts and alcoholics, and I pointed out some of the men to them. "Arabs and Jews live here," I said. "We teach the Bible, and believe that Jesus is the Messiah. If you come here, you will have to get up at 6:00 a.m., make your bed, pray, and be at breakfast at 7:00 a.m., or you won't get any breakfast," I challenged them. "You see that rough-looking worker over there?" I asked.

"Yes," they said.

"He's an ex-addict and an ex-Marine from New York." I laid it on the line. "He's tough. If you don't get up on time, he'll throw a bucket of water on you. This place is like boot camp; it's basic training for drug addicts. If you lived here, we would make you go to school, and you'd have to do your homework. And worst of all, everyone who lives here has to wash dishes. That means you, too. So, you don't want to live here, do you?" I waited for their response.

The two boys stared at me. Then David, the younger of the two, said, "We can do it!"

"Yeah, we can do it," Ron agreed.

My heart began to melt. I wanted to help these two precious boys. I showed them around the grounds and the house and introduced them to several of the staff. I told the boys to think about it and that I would talk it over with our staff and get back to them.

When I returned home Karen asked me about the two boys. I choked up and started crying. Finally I said, "We need to take them in. It's a critical moment in their lives. The Lord wants to rescue them before it's too late."

"But two boys living with these other men?" Karen questioned me. "David, are you sure you're hearing from God?" she asked.

"Yes, I'm sure. The staff will be like big brothers to them," I assured her. "These kids need family, and that's what we're supposed to be, isn't it?"

I met with the staff and told them what I sensed was the Lord's will. "I don't know anything about working with teenagers," one staff member said.

"Neither do I," I replied. "The Lord will show us."

Tanneken, our cook and women's counselor, wondered if this was the best thing for the boys. Again I quoted Isaiah 58, saying we were, "to bring the homeless poor into the house." We prayed together, and I called Tony in Kiryat Shmonah. "Tony," I said, "bring Ron and David to House of Victory. Let's just trust the Lord on this one."

On *Yom Ha'atzmaut*, Israel's Independence Day, Tony and his family brought Ron and David to live at House of Victory. We had a barbecue with the staff and students that day, and I think the boys thought we lived like that every day! They moved into a small bedroom and began to adapt to the new world that had opened up for them.

Danny Sayag took Ron and David to register in a local school as their "uncle." Each day Eddie, the House of Victory dog, waited anxiously at the door for Ron to come home from school. The two boys did their homework with staff members, and even the students in the program began to help them. Like everyone else in the house, they had chores to do. They even washed the dreaded dishes when it was their turn. Of course, they especially enjoyed recreation days when they played soccer or basketball with the staff and students.

Ron and David began to attend the prayer meetings and worship services in the house and at Stella Carmel. Burt Singer, an evangelist in the congregation, and his wife Pam encouraged them to surrender their lives to Jesus. The boys realized that what they were hearing preached and taught was the truth. Several weeks after they moved into House of Victory, they were baptized on the Haifa beach. When I asked David why he wanted to be baptized, he answered, "So I can love my brother more."

In July, the boys joined the Youth With A Mission (YWAM) "King's Kids" camp for a month. A Swiss doctor and his wife brought the program to Israel and about thirty Arab, Jewish, and European teens joined it at Stella Carmel. They learned to have "a quiet time" with the Lord each morning and how to work with others as a team. The King's Kids learned to sing a number of praise and worship songs and to dance to some as well. When they were ready, the team of young people were taken to perform and witness in Arab churches and schools in Galilee and in Messianic congregations in Haifa, Tiberias, Jaffa, and Jerusalem.

Just before Ron and David went off to King's Kids, we invited them to spend a weekend with us in our apartment, which was located about ten minutes away from House of Victory. Late that night, as the boys were asleep in our little guest room, Karen and I were unable to sleep. Soon, more addicts would be arriving at House of Victory, and the beds in the boys' room would be needed. We were deeply concerned about their situation and knew that what the boys needed was security and a home. Laying in bed, we stared at each other. We both knew in our hearts what the Lord was saying to us. We'd never had children of our own. But now we believed that He was giving us these two boys, and we were going to be their mother and father.

The following week after a Shabbat meeting at Stella Carmel, Karen and I sat down with Ron and David on the veranda overlooking Galilee. I told them there was something important we wanted to discuss with them.

"Boys," I began, "we've been praying about your situation. It's not really the best thing for you to stay at House of Victory. We think the Lord wants us to serve as your parents." They just stared at us. "As you finish King's Kids, Karen and I will be moving into a new apartment. You could help us move and come live with us. We can start living as a family before school starts. What do you think about the idea?"

They looked at us and then at each other. David said to Ron, "Well, you know what I've always said."

"What have you always said?" I asked him.

"Wherever he goes, I go," David answered, nodding toward his big brother.

"I'll tell you what," I said. "You boys talk it over and pray about it. Next Shabbat we'll meet with you again and we'll see how the Lord is leading us. Okay?"

"Okay," they agreed. Then we prayed together that the Lord would show us His perfect will and help us all to follow it.

During the middle of the week, I went to Stella Carmel and I ran into Ron. I asked him how he was doing. He smiled. "God's preparing my heart," he said.

The following Shabbat we met with the boys again. "Did you hear from God?" I asked them.

They both nodded their heads. "Yes, we did," they said. There was a long pause, as the four of us looked at each other.

"Well, what did He say?" Karen finally blurted out. There was another pause.

Then very slowly, David replied, "God said, Y-E-S." We hugged each other and prayed together. God was blessing us in a way we never could even have imagined!

When the King's Kids camp ended, Ron and "Little" David moved into the new apartment that we had just rented, around the corner from our old apartment where they had spent the night with us. They had a large room of their own. Our living room had a magnificent view looking across a nature reserve to the sea. Each evening, we were treated to a glorious sunset. Karen had a little prayer room attached to our bedroom, which the Lord knew she would need, and I had a small study where we put a single bed for visitors. Ron, who has artistic ability, helped Karen hang paintings and decorate the apartment.

Our lives changed radically. Overnight, we were transformed from a couple who treasured their privacy, into the parents of two active, growing, wounded boys. I watched my wife blossom into a loving, understanding Jewish mother. In the meantime, the Lord sent two women to work in the House of Victory office. Karen had set up and managed the office, but now she was released to be a mother. The Lord showed me that as I fathered these boys, He would keep our congregation on track. He didn't just want teachers, He wanted fathers who could be godly examples for our children. I had prayed "make me a pastor." Now, I prayed "make me a father." I was learning that they're really one and the same.

Soon after the boys moved in with us, we became their legal foster parents. The social workers who had been involved with Ron and David were curious to visit House of Victory as they began to learn more about us. One morning, three social workers, two Jewish women and one Arab woman, met with our staff and students. Several men explained how they had been bound by drugs or alcohol for years. Each one's story was different, but they all had one thing in common. They now believed in Yeshua as their Savior, had repented, and had received the Holy Spirit. They explained that the program was Bible study and prayer. One of the social workers asked if we did family counseling with the parents, wives, and children of the addicts. I told her that we did. "What do you counsel them?" she asked.

"We help them to understand the principles of the Bible, the Word of God," I answered. "We explain what the Bible teaches about marriage and the family."

The Arab social worker asked one of the Jewish students, "You believe in Jesus, and you're a Jew? I have never heard of such a thing."

"Jesus was a Jew," Daniel replied. "He's our Messiah."

Raja, one of the Arab men in the program, said that he had learned to love Jews at House of Victory. His wife, he said, was shocked to see him wash dishes when he came home for a weekend because Arab men don't wash dishes. "Maybe I should send my husband here!" the Arab social worker laughed.

One of the women asked if we did music therapy. "Yes, we do," Danny Sayag answered and began to sing in Hebrew:

> "Give thanks to the Lord, for He is good!
> For His mercy endures forever"
> (Ps. 118:1 NKJ).

Soon we were all singing, Jews and Arabs together. The sweet presence of the Holy Spirit was manifested in the room. The head social worker whispered to Karen that her Orthodox Jewish father had always said that what they needed in their home was the presence of God. Then she said, "God is in this place."

Some time after the social workers' visit, the Social Services office of the City of Haifa launched a campaign to inform the public about the growing need for foster parents. As they began to design the posters and flyers that would be distributed, they asked if they could interview us along with several other families, and we agreed. Much to our surprise, the only picture that appeared on the posters and flyers was a color picture of Karen and me, with a headline above it in Hebrew: "We are a Foster Family. And you?" These large, full-color posters were hung all over Haifa in shopping malls, clinics, and synagogues. People now recognize us from the posters. As a result, many doors have opened for us to testify about our Lord.

Karen and I have been blessed to minister together in Finland, Switzerland, Germany, and England. We thank God for the ongoing support from the precious believers in these countries that makes the program at House of Victory possible.

In 1995, we also ministered in congregations throughout Holland, where I preached on "The Spirit and Power of Elijah." While we were in Amsterdam, I met with the producer of a TV show at the Evangelical Broadcasting Station and told him about our work in Israel. The producers decided to send a team to Israel to make a video about House of Victory.

On the video, Karen and I retraced our steps to Frida's door in the Old City of Jerusalem, where we first heard about the drug problem. Graduates of our program testified to the transforming power of God's grace. When the program aired in Holland, the producer called us to say that it was very well-received. In fact, they had footage left over, and they wanted to produce a second one. David Wilkerson agreed to endorse the ministry on the second video. The viewers of these two showings on Dutch TV contributed enough money for House of Victory to purchase two new vans, a computer, a fax machine, and new furniture for the meeting room and office. The videos are now in English and German as well.

We were overwhelmed by God's "double blessing." What God initiates, He supports. "The Lord gives grace and glory; no good thing does He withhold from those who walk uprightly" (Ps. 84:11).

Chapter 14

The Spirit & Power of Elijah

As we went about the Lord's work on Mount Carmel, I often taught on "the spirit of Elijah." To my surprise, the same old enemies of the purposes of God who attacked Elijah were still around and surfaced again. When the enemy could not abort the birth of House of Victory and Carmel Assembly, he tried another of his age-old tactics—infiltration. In answer to our fervent prayers that the "Lord of the harvest" would thrust out laborers, He sent some very precious people to co-labor with us. However, there were others, who arrived on Mount Carmel, who clearly were not sent by God. After several were unmasked, I realized that they all had three things in common. First, none of them had been biblically sent out by a local congregation. Second, although they were working with us, they never actually became accountable to our congregation. Finally, as in the case of several couples, the woman was usually the dominating influence in the marriage. As in the time of Elijah, we were under a vicious, full-scale attack from the controlling spirit of Jezebel, aided and abetted by her weak consort, Ahab.

These attacks on the body are not new. They have been going on since the birth of the Church. Paul warned the leaders of the church at Ephesus: "Be on guard for yourselves and for all the flock, among which the Holy Spirit has made you overseers, to shepherd the church of God, which He purchased with His own blood. I know that... savage wolves will come in among you, not sparing the flock" (Acts 20:28-29). Paul told the God-appointed leaders that these people would arise from "among your own selves" in order "to draw away the disciples after them" (Acts 20:30). That is just what some of these "wolves in sheep's clothing" attempted to do.

Jesus Himself, "the Son of God, who has eyes like a flame of fire," chastised the powerful church at Thyatira and warned them in His letter that He had one thing against them: "...You tolerate the woman Jezebel, who calls herself a prophetess, and she teaches and leads My bond-servants astray...I gave her time to repent; and she does not want to repent" (Rev. 2:20-21).

Some of these people appeared so kind and sweet that, initially, we were deceived into thinking God had sent them. We were desperate for help because of all the needy people who came to us, and our desperation blinded us. Later, the rotten fruit would manifest in their lives. One woman said her "ministry" was to tell well-known men of God what was wrong with their ministry. She hardly ever stopped talking, and her husband was silent as a tomb. When she arrived, she said she had some kind of throat infection and asked me to pray for her. I agreed, and laid hands on her. I realized later that I should not have done that, because whatever spirit was on her, attacked me. As I walked back to my chair, I almost fell down. She was healed, but the next day I could hardly talk. I ended up in the hospital doubled-over with pain, while this couple, who had come "to help," were trying to take over God's ministry. The doctors never found out what was wrong with me, but I knew. We had come against the "spirit of Jezebel," the same one that made Elijah run for his life.

These "Jezebels" wore many masks. One couple had an overt religious spirit. The "prophetess" wife gave a vicious, false word to a couple that severely wounded them. Of course, when confronted, this woman would not repent.

The various people also used a variety of techniques. One clever trick was to become someone's "prayer partner." This sounded very good. Who could be against prayer? However, the naive participant would then open her ears to all the poison the "current Jezebel" spewed out. It would contaminate both of them, and the disease would spread.

One "nice" lady seemed to have "words" for almost everybody. She would sidle up behind someone and slip a little piece of paper into his or her hand. Then, she would smile and purr, "God gave me this for you." These "words" were almost always off base, and they were often in direct opposition to what the Spirit was really saying to His flock.

A year before we left New York, the Lord was really blessing our precious times of intercession in the prayer meeting we had started for Israel at Times Square Church. However, two women joined our meetings, and it became clear to me that their motives were not pure. They were personally ambitious. They both brought disturbing messages to Karen, some of which were intended to discourage her from our plans to move to Israel. One night after a service, I was near the stage of the Nederlander Theatre.

As I started to walk up the aisle toward the back of the theatre, these two seemingly sweet, gentle ladies stood shoulder to shoulder at the top of the aisle, smiling at me. I'd
seen them walking around the theatre physically stroking
people. Now, as I slowly walked toward them, I suddenly
had a vision of them as two hideous, slimy, black pythons.
Shocked, I slipped into a seat, dropped to my knees, and
began to pray. After a time, I got up and the women were
gone. Later, I confronted both of them and did not allow
Karen to receive their calls anymore. Some months afterward, one of these women tried to usurp another woman's
ministry. The second married a man who had been mightily used by God. He is no longer in ministry.

"Jezebel" has always gone after God's "point men."
These are men and women whom He appoints to raise
up new works. This spirit hates the true prophetic calling
and ministry as Jezebel did. They cannot accept that it is
God Himself who "...has placed the members, each one of
them, in the body, just as He desired...God has appointed
in the church, first apostles, second prophets, third teachers..." (1 Cor. 12:18,28). Since we were the vessels He had
chosen to use to plant and lead these new works in Haifa,
Karen and I became the main targets of the enemy coun-
terattack. One consistent stream of accusation was, "Their
message of holiness is too hard." People were told not to
listen to the message of repentance that we preached.

Once, we allowed a young lady, who was a student at
House of Victory, to spend the weekend with a couple in
our congregation. This Jewish woman had been delivered
from years of heroin addiction and had become a believer.
Her hard character was starting to soften and change. She
was at a very sensitive point in the process of being healed
from the devastation caused by years of a degrading
lifestyle. Her difficult personality had already exhausted

five women counselors. While she was visiting with this couple, the wife, who dominated her weak husband, invited a "prophetess" friend to "minister" to her without our knowledge.

When our young lady returned, she had regressed back into her hard shell of bitterness, anger, and unforgiveness. Her old, destructive attitudes and patterns of behavior had returned. She had been told not to listen to us and to our staff—the ones who had taken her in when her life was in danger. We had fed, clothed, loved, taught, and poured ourselves out for her for months. Instead, she had been deceived by a "lone wolf," and had dined at "Jezebel's table" on a poisonous meal of false prophecies covered over with large helpings of "sloppy agape." She was encouraged to continue in her old, self-destructive ways. By offering her carnal sympathy, they "enabled" her to stay stuck in her patterns of behavior.

Jesus has solemn words for those who cause His sheep to stray and fall: "But whoever causes one of these little ones who believe in Me to stumble, it is better for him that a heavy millstone be hung around his neck, and that he be drowned in the depth of the sea" (Mt. 18:6).

The Jezebel/Ahab pattern was also manifested in a pastoral couple we knew. Some young people in this pastor's youth group were practicing sexual immorality, and many in their church knew about it. The pastor had been confronted about the situation by at least three witnesses, including me, because he had invited me to minister there. I told him that he had to deal with the sin in his camp, or he would be like Eli, the priest, who refused to rebuke his sons when they committed sexual sin in the doorway of the tent of meeting (see 1 Sam. 2:22). He refused to even admit what was happening and accused me of being judgmental. This couple is no longer in Israel. This situation was a warning to us that God would remove compromised leadership.

I was learning not to react to the Jezebel spirit in the flesh, but instead to simply go to the Lord in prayer. Controlling spirits must be dealt with in the spirit realm. In the first several years of our ministry here, there were a dozen or so "Jezebel" episodes. Each time I prayed, "Lord, if they won't repent, remove them. Your Word says don't tolerate them. Take them somewhere else where they will do no damage." Several times the spiritual pressure was so intimidating and oppressive that I felt like giving up, just as Elijah did. But then the Lord in His faithfulness delivered us each time.

In the spring of 1996, I was invited to Britain for a "Prayer For Israel" conference and ministry tour. I was asked to speak on "The Sound of the Abundance of Rain" (1 Kings 18:41 NKJ), which dealt with the future revival I see coming to Galilee, Mount Carmel, and Lebanon. While I was there, the Lord impressed upon me that He was pleased that we had not tolerated the "spirit of Jezebel," but now He wanted to show me another key to His promised revival in northern Israel. His message, simply, was this: "Confront Ahab."

I began to study the character of this evil king. In First Kings 18:1 (NKJ) the Lord said to Elijah, "Go, present yourself to Ahab, and I will send rain." Elijah, a sojourner (pilgrim) from Gilead, courageously confronted Ahab who "did more to provoke the Lord God of Israel to anger than all the kings of Israel who were before him" (1 Kings 16: 33 NKJ).

Ahab was responsible for popularizing and promoting the abominable worship practices of the false god, Baal. He gave his official governmental approval to child sacrifice, temple prostitution, homosexuality, and nature worship, all of which took root on Mount Carmel and in northern Israel. He married Jezebel, an occult priestess, who set out to systematically slaughter God's true prophets. Jezebel set up her own pseudo-religious system, for which Ahab built her a temple in Samaria (the so-called West Bank).

As I studied the words and actions of this weak, backslidden husband, father, and leader, I began to understand why God was so angry with him. Ahab reeked of carnality, compromise, covetousness, and spiritual cowardice.

This energetic, popular, and successful warrior was the epitome of the man of flesh. Continually, he operated out of his own feelings, fears, and soulish desires. "The carnal mind is enmity against God" (Rom. 8:7 NKJ). This enemy of God was easily seduced, and he longed for the popular approval of man. Ahab might have looked impressive in his robes or armor, but inside he was a spiritual wimp who was manipulated by an ambitious, seductive wife.

"Ahabs" abdicate their God-given, God-commanded responsibilities as husbands, fathers, or leaders. The Ahab spirit permeates the world and has penetrated the body of Christ. "Ahabs" shirk their place as the priest, whose job it is to pray for his household. They wrongly leave spiritual leadership up to their wives. These men are the architects of a "fatherless generation," and they are largely responsible for the worldwide epidemics of divorce and abortion.

"Ahabs" are the plague of godly wives. Their minds are set on the things of the world, rather than the rigorous study and application of God's Holy Word. Some I have known love to "major in minors." They are more inter-ested in titillating themselves with peripheral and faddish doctrines than in concentrating on developing godly character. Some do not eat the solid food of the Word, so they never grow up. Rather, they remain immature and childish—not child-like. When they refuse to change, they only grow worse.

Because Ahab was carnal, his spiritual life was compro-mised. Ahab is essentially the *man of mixture*. He refuses to distinguish between the holy and the profane, and jeal-ously guards an unholy alliance with his old nature. Men like Ahab operate in the soul realm of their feelings or intellect, and they eventually become deceived, think-ing that they are moving in the Spirit. Ahab mistakenly thought Elijah was the "troubler of Israel," when actually he himself was the problem.

These weak men deny the transforming power of the true gospel, and reject the message of the cross and the crucified life. Their foundations are shaky, so they are unstable, tossed to and fro like a cork in the ocean. They are reeds blowing in every "wind of doctrine." "Ahabs" are stubborn and fearfully cling to the false security of their old, carnal identities. They do not want to pay the price of the slow, steady formation of Christ-like character, which can only be attained by dying daily to our old nature and consistently obeying the Word of God.

Although he already possessed wealth, Ahab could never get enough. He lusted after his neighbor's vineyard, another man's inheritance, in flagrant defiance of the Word of God. When godly Naboth wouldn't give his lawful possession to the king, Ahab sulked like a child. Jezebel at-tacked her husband's manhood with her words, and then she and her "religious" crowd put on a show. She wrote letters in Ahab's name, proclaimed a fast, and brought in some false witnesses. First, she assassinated Naboth's character; then she had him assassinated, cloaking it all in religious fervor.

I believe religious evil is the most displeasing, dishonoring, and repugnant sin to a holy God. Jesus reacted in righteous indignation to religious hypocrites and they killed Him out of envy. When you envy someone, coveting that person's possessions, whether it's their vineyard, their money, their ministry, or their anointing, it really means that you want that person out of your way. In truth, jealousy is murderous: "Where jealousy and selfish ambition exist, there is disorder and every evil thing" (James 3:16). In leaders like Ahab, whose authority is mixed with insecurity, the mixture will be disastrous. Their decisions will never be sound or consistent; instead, they will move in confusion. "God is not the author of confusion" (1 Cor. 14:33 NKJ).

How did God react to compromising, covetous Ahab? He sent His man, Elijah, to confront the king in his sin in the very vineyard that Ahab thought that he now possessed. Elijah didn't mince any words with the murderous thief. The prophet told him that in that vineyard "dogs shall lick up your blood…because you have sold yourself to do evil in the sight of the Lord" (1 Kings 21:19-20). (The false religion that Ahab and Jezebel promoted revered dogs. They allowed them to lick human wounds because they believed that dog saliva had healing power!)

Ahab's children also died because of their father's sin. Instead of training his children in righteousness, he contaminated them with his idolatry. His deplorable life is a strong example of ungodliness to us all: a weak husband, father, and leader ruled by compromise who refused to take a stand for God.

Ahab's carnality and compromise also led to his cowardice. In his war against Syria, he made an unholy alliance with King Jehoshaphat. He told Jehoshaphat, "I will disguise myself and go into the battle, but you put on your robes" (1 Kings 22:30). Jehoshaphat almost died in the battle, but God saved him when he prayed. Ahab, however, died that day, even though he was disguised, and the dogs licked up his blood at Naboth's place.

"Ahabs" do not fight fair. They are sneaky and secretive, hiding from the light. However, there is an antidote to the Ahab spirit.

The opposite spirit of Ahab and Jezebel is "the spirit of Elijah." Many think that "the spirit of Elijah" involves becoming a tough, old prophet who calls down the fire of God's judgment, as Elijah did on Mount Carmel. However, when James and John, "the Sons of Thunder," wanted "to command fire to come down from heaven and consume" a Samaritan village that would not receive Jesus, the Lord "…turned and rebuked them, and said, 'You do not know what kind of spirit you are of; for the Son of man did not come to destroy men's lives, but to save them'" (Lk. 9:55-56a). As I have studied the Scriptures, I have found that "the spirit of Elijah" is something quite different from what James and John originally thought.

Two thousand years ago, an elderly, devout, childless priest went into the temple in Jerusalem to burn incense at the hour of prayer. To his amazement, Zacharias heard an angel of the Lord tell him that he and his wife Elizabeth would have a son and that they should name him John. The angel said that:

"For he will be great in the sight of the Lord, and shall drink neither wine nor strong drink. He will also be filled with the Holy Spirit, even from his mother's womb. And he will turn many of the children of Israel to the Lord their God. He will also go before Him in the spirit and power of Elijah, 'to turn the hearts of the fathers to the children,' and the disobedient to the wisdom of the just, to make ready a people prepared for the Lord" (Lk. 1:15-17 NKJ).

Our call on Mount Carmel is "to turn the children of Israel to the Lord their God" and "to make ready a people prepared for the Lord." Elijah and John the Baptist, who moved in the "spirit and power of Elijah," are examples for us today.

John the Baptist, who came in "the spirit of Elijah," was "great in the sight of the Lord," not great in his own eyes. When the priests and Levites flocked to the revival at the Jordan that John had ushered in, they asked him, "Who are you? Elijah, the Prophet, the Christ (Messiah)?" He merely answered them, "I am a voice of one crying in the wilderness, 'MAKE STRAIGHT THE WAY OF THE LORD'" (see Jn. 1:19-23).

John was not interested in status, or being great in the sight of man. He didn't need a title. It was John who said, "A man can receive nothing, unless it has been given him from heaven" (Jn. 3:27). John called himself "the friend of the bridegroom" (Jn. 3:29). He said, "He [Jesus] must increase, but I must decrease" (Jn. 3:30). The humble prophet announced to the crowds, who thronged around him in expectation of the Messiah: "…As for me, I baptize you with water; but One is coming who is mightier than I, and I am not fit to untie the thong of His sandals; He will baptize you with the Holy Spirit and fire" (Lk. 3:16).

After four hundred years of silence, God began to speak. John exploded from the desert as the voice of God at one of the darkest hours of Israel's tragic history.

In the dark time of Elijah, there had been half a century of idolatry with six successive, wicked kings preceding Ahab. With corrupt leaders, a backslidden priesthood, and official governmental endorsement of gross sin, the cycle of evil had reached its peak. Into this arena stepped one man who knew his God. His first words are the key to his character: "...As the Lord the God of Israel lives, before whom I stand..." (1 Kings 17:1). Elijah (meaning "Jehovah is my God") stood up in righteousness for his God.

After Elijah prophesied the terrible judgment of drought upon the land, the Lord said to him, "hide yourself by the brook Cherith" (1 Kings 17:3). For a whole year the prophet communed with his Lord, drinking from the brook of His Spirit and being fed daily, supernaturally, by bread and meat that God supplied. As the armies of Ahab searched for Elijah, he humbled himself and waited upon the Lord, totally dependent on His protection and provision. God gives grace to the humble, to the lowly ones walking in child-like faith. These are the ones God will use to raise up His holy standard against the carnal, compromising spirit of Ahab.

When the brook dried up, the Lord spoke a very clear word to Elijah: "Arise, go to Zarephath, which belongs to Sidon, and stay there; behold, I have commanded a widow there to provide for you" (1 Kings 17:9). The Hebrew name Zarephath means "refining." The Lord wanted to purify His prophet, to purge away dross and mixture from his character. Not only that, but God commanded him to go to Jezebel's hometown, the occult capital of the Middle

East. Elijah, the Jew, was told to live with a heathen widow! What would we have done? Would we have made excuses or argued with God? Perhaps we would have asked, "Why?" Not Elijah. Two verbs show us the character of this man. He "arose" and "went" (1 Kings 17:10). He displayed instant obedience. No arguments, just obedience. The "spirit of Elijah" is rooted in humility and obedience. He willingly went to the place of refining. Elijah's spirit, his innermost being, was "hidden with Christ in God."

The Jewish prophet went to a heathen town and a heathen home where the Lord took him through another season of heart preparation. Israel's most wanted man was living on the devil's doorstep. For two years, day by day, week by week, month after long month, Elijah lived with a widow and her son. God consistently and miraculously provided for their daily needs. Godly character was being worked into this man. I believe his humility of spirit is the key to the power that God was about to release through him. God had found and molded someone He could trust.

Then tragedy struck: "Now it came about after these things, that the son of the woman, the mistress of the house, became sick; and his sickness was so severe, that there was no breath left in him" (1 Kings 17:17). The widow in her grief blamed Elijah. And how did the prophet respond?

> "And he said to her, 'Give me your son.' Then he took him from her bosom and carried him up to the upper room where he was living, and laid him on his own bed...Then he stretched himself upon the child three times, and called to the Lord, and said, 'O Lord my God, I pray Thee, let this child's life return to him'" (1 Kings 17:19,21).

Elijah was being stretched to identify with the misery and death of individuals who were not his own flesh. He willingly "stretched himself" into a place of intercession that he had never before experienced.

When the Lord gave Karen and me our two precious, foster sons, He spoke very specifically to me. He said He wanted "more than a prophet," the words Jesus had used to describe John the Baptist (Mt. 11:9). Our oldest boy Ron's full name is "Yeshurun," one of the biblical names of Israel. The Lord told me that Ron represented the people of Israel. If I could not love and minister to this wounded, young man, I could not minister to His people Israel. The "spirit of Elijah" turns "the hearts of the fathers back to the children."

With child-like faith Elijah prayed a simple prayer. "And the Lord heard the voice of Elijah, and the life of the child returned to him and he revived" (1 Kings 17:22). It was "life from the dead" through the intercession of one godly man. The prophet picked up the boy and carried him down the steps. Imagine the mother's face as Elijah gave the boy back to her and said, "See, your son is alive" (1 Kings 17:23). I have seen the tear-stained faces of mothers who have looked upon their sons who have been delivered from the death-grip of drugs. The "spirit of Elijah" is the spirit of the "Good Samaritan," the spirit of one who will pour himself out for others. It is the spirit of Jesus.

The proven and tested prophet was now ready for his mountaintop assignment—a public confrontation with a false religious system. Once again he went to confront Ahab and told the king to his face: "…You have forsaken the commandments of the Lord, and you have followed the Baals. Now then send and gather to me all Israel on Mount Carmel, together with four hundred and fifty prophets of Baal and four hundred prophets of the Asherah, who eat at Jezebel's table" (1 Kings 18:18-19).

What a scene it must have been on the top of Mount Carmel as families from all over Israel joined Ahab's glittering army and 850 false prophets in all their gaudy religious paraphernalia. Then one lone man appeared. Girded about his loins was a leather belt and hung around his shoulders was an old hairy cloak—the cloak of a prophet. As Elijah courageously confronted the society of his day, he asked his people the only question that has ever mattered: "How long will you hesitate between two opinions? If the Lord is God, follow Him; but if Baal, follow him" (1 Kings 18:21a). As Elijah stared at the multitude, a holy hush fell on the mountaintop. Not one person dared to answer. How the prophet's heart must have ached. Not one would choose to follow the God of Abraham, Isaac, and Jacob!

Elijah proposed a contest between him and Baal's prophets. He suggested that the prophets of Baal cut up an ox and place it upon wood on an altar, and then call on the name of their god. He would do the same and call on the name of the Lord (Jehovah). Then he said, " 'The God who answers by fire, He is God.' And all the people answered and said, 'That is a good idea'" (1 Kings 18:24b).

The contest went on most of the day, as the false prophets screamed and leaped and danced about the altar they had made. The noise and frenzy got wilder and wilder as they cut themselves with swords and raved and "prophesied." "But there was no voice, no one answered, and no one paid attention" (1 Kings 18:29b).

Finally, "Elijah said to all the people, 'Come near to me.' So all the people came near to him. And he repaired the altar of the Lord which had been torn down" (1 Kings 18:30). Slowly, he carried the twelve stones, representing restoration, unity, and completion of the twelve tribes of Israel, as he rebuilt the place of sacrifice to the one true God. He arranged the wood, then he cut up an ox and put its bloody pieces on the wood. Three times they poured water all over the altar. The people must have watched the prophet in breathless anticipation as he came near to the altar and spoke to his God:

> "'O Lord, the God of Abraham, Isaac and Israel, today let it be known that Thou art God in Israel, and that I am Thy servant, and that I have done all these things at Thy word. Answer me, O Lord, answer me, that this people may know that Thou, O Lord, art God, and that Thou hast turned their heart back again.' Then the fire of the Lord fell, and consumed the burnt offering and the wood and the stones and the dust, and licked up the water that was in the trench" (1 Kings 18:36-38).

God had accepted the sacrifice! Holy fire had fallen! Everything burned from top to bottom—even the stones were consumed! And now how did the people respond? "When all the people saw it, they fell on their faces; and they said, 'The Lord, He is God; the Lord, He is God'" (1 Kings 18:39b).

After the dramatic defeat and destruction of the false prophets, Ahab and his comrades indulged themselves in the traditional post-sacrificial meal and celebration, but not Elijah. His work wasn't finished. "So Ahab went up to eat and drink. But Elijah went up to the top of Carmel; and he crouched down on the earth, and put his face between his knees" (1 Kings 18:42). What a contrast Elijah was to the religious, self-righteous man, who feasted and caroused just after the god he worshiped had been exposed as worthless and false.

Here, we have a powerful picture of two kinds of believers. Ahab's group had just confessed that Jehovah was God, but they went right back to "business as usual." God's man, Elijah, was on his face communing with his Lord. Only he heard what the Lord was about to do. Only he heard the approaching "sound of abundance of rain" (1 Kings 18:41 NKJ), while those who were dining at Ahab's and Jezebel's table heard only the noise of carnality, compromise, and confusion.

Elijah told his servant to go up and look toward the sea. The man reported that he could see nothing. Seven times the prophet told him to go up and look, while Elijah remained on his face, bent over, interceding with God. He had separated himself from Ahab's compromising world— a world partying toward the abyss. The carnal atmosphere of accommodating the flesh will always be fatal to the life of the spirit.

Jesus said, "But you, when you pray, go into your [inner] room, and when you have shut your door [turned off the phone and TV], pray to your Father who is in the secret place; and your Father who sees in secret will reward you openly" (Mt. 6:6 NKJ). Elijah was in "the secret place," pleading for the rain that God had promised.

As he prayed for the promised rain, his prayer was specific and persistent. Persistence breaks resistance. The seventh time (the number seven signifies completion) his servant went up and saw "a cloud, as small as a man's hand, rising out of the sea!" (1 Kings 18:44 NKJ). The Hebrew word translated as "cloud" here means "a man's palm." Elijah was raising his palm in supplication for his people according to God's will and promise. The result: a DOWN-POUR of rain, after three and a half years of drought.

Here is the commentary from the New Testament:

> "Elijah was a man with a nature like ours, and he prayed earnestly that it would not rain; and it did not rain on the land for three years and six months. And he prayed again, and the heaven gave rain, and the earth produced its fruit" (James 5:17-18 NKJ).

The "spirit of Elijah" is upon those who consistently "go up" into the Lord's presence in intercession and don't let go of God until the answer comes. "The effective, fervent prayer of a righteous man avails much" (James 5:16b NKJ). This was one of the first Scriptures I memorized as a young believer, but I had left out the first half of this verse: "Confess your trespasses to one another, and pray for one another, that you may be healed." We all want to avoid daily repentance and accountability, but if we desire to move in "the spirit of Elijah" we must be clean before God. The Lord's promise to answer our prayers is conditional: "And whatever we ask we receive from Him, because we keep His commandments and do the things that are pleasing in His sight" (1 Jn. 3:22).

Have you heard the rain recently? Are you separated to Him in humility? Do you continue to "go up" to the "secret place"? Are you obeying His Word and doing the things pleasing in His sight? Your public ministry will only be as powerful as your private prayer life. This is the "spirit and power of Elijah."

The lasting legacy of Elijah was not to call fire down on the mountain, nor was it to pray for the rain that came, or even to raise a boy from the dead. None of these miraculous activities ultimately turned the children of Israel back to their God.

After the Lord's great victory on Mount Carmel Elijah ran from Jezebel. The Scripture is clear: "He was afraid, and ran for his life" (1 Kings 19:3). The Hebrew word used for "his life" is *nafsho*, or "his soul." I believe this great man, in his exhaustion and disappointment, faltered and began to function in the soul realm, rather than in the Spirit. God didn't give him the spirit of fear. He should have confronted Jezebel there at Jezreel, where "the hand of the Lord" had taken him (1 Kings 18:46). Nonetheless, the Lord in His mercy fed the discouraged prophet and led him to a cave to talk to him. As Elijah wrapped himself in his old prophet's mantle (the root of which in Hebrew means "glory" or "majesty") in the entrance to the cave, he heard the Lord's voice again. God told him to anoint Jehu as king and Elisha as the prophet to replace him (see 1 Kings 19:16). These two men would finish the work Elijah had begun. Jehu, indeed, destroyed Jezebel.

Elijah obeyed the Lord, found Elisha ("My God saves"), and threw his prophet's mantle over the young man. Elisha began to follow Elijah, ministering to and serving his new master. For about seven years, the old prophet poured himself into Elisha, the spiritual son whom God had given Elijah to help him complete the Lord's work. Together, they raised up schools of prophets on Mount Carmel, at Bethel, Gilgal, and Jericho. The enduring legacy of Elijah is to be found in these training schools, where they made disciples who became the salt and light in the surrounding darkness. By upholding the Lord's standards, these disciples held back God's righteous judgment on Israel for decades.

When the Lord was ready to take Elijah home, Elisha would not leave his side. The master and his inseparable disciple went to the Jordan River, but the others stayed back. "Now fifty men of the sons of the prophets went and stood opposite them at a distance, while the two of them stood by the Jordan" (2 Kings 2:7). When Elijah struck the Jordan with his mantle, the river opened up and the two of them crossed over on dry ground. It was then that Elisha asked Elijah for a double portion of his spirit. Elijah answered, "You have asked a hard thing. Nevertheless, if you see me when I am taken from you, it shall be so" (2 Kings 2:10). Then they walked and talked together. I've often wondered what the father and his son discussed. The fifty who held back missed the intimacy that Elisha enjoyed. He was the only one who crossed over the Jordan with Elijah.

All of a sudden Elijah was caught up in the whirlwind to heaven. As his father was taken from him: "Elisha saw it and cried out, 'My father, my father, the chariots of Israel and its horsemen!'" (2 Kings 2:12). Elijah was gone.

Elisha tore his clothes in anguish. As he wept, he saw something lying on the ground. It was the mantle of Elijah that had fallen from him. Elisha humbly picked up the old, hairy cloak. Finally, he walked back to the Jordan River. As he took the cloak and "struck the waters, they were divided here and there, and Elisha crossed over" (2 Kings 2:14b). The fifty other sons of the prophets who were watching said, "The spirit of Elijah rests on Elisha" (2 Kings 2:15).

The "double blessing" is the inheritance given to the firstborn son. It is also the imperishable and undefiled inheritance reserved for all who are willing to completely surrender to Jesus. "The Spirit Himself bears witness with our spirit that we are children of God, and if children, heirs also, heirs of God and fellow heirs with Christ, if indeed we suffer with Him in order that we may also be glorified with Him" (Rom. 8:16-17).

Chapter 15

Restoring the Altar of the Lord

A number of years ago, I served as the artistic director for two newly constructed theatres and was also involved in designing a new theatre for the university where I had worked. The new theatre had been a dream of mine for years, but it was never built. Now, the Lord was calling us to build a house of worship on the top of Mount Carmel. I realized He had prepared me for the task and He was giving me my heart's desire: "Delight yourself in the Lord; and He will give you the desires of your heart" (Ps. 37:4).

As a theatre director, I would study a play for months, trying to discern its deepest meanings, its essence. Then I would hire a team of artists–scenery, lighting, costume, and sound designers. We would come together to discuss the meaning and imagery of the script, and then, through our combined skills and imaginations, we would try to create our vision of the play. I must have participated in thousands of production meetings in my twenty-five years in the theatre and television.

Though building a congregational house of worship would not be inspired by self, we knew we needed just the right team to create the vision that the Lord would inspire. We began to pray that the Lord would form a building team of believers. Philip, a Messianic Jew, was selected as our architect, and Rizik, an Arab Christian from Nazareth, was hired as the engineer. Mike, a Jewish believer from our congregation who owns a construction company, became the construction manager. Gerald, an Assemblies of God builder from the United States, and his wife Jane just "happened" to be working in Israel at the time and attending Carmel Assembly. Gerald had built buildings for Assemblies' ministries in different parts of the world. His denomination graciously "loaned" him to us to serve as our building project supervisor. The Lord also sent us Teresa, another Messianic Jew, to manage the finances during the construction of the worship center.

The building team began to meet to discuss the project and pray about it. As we sought the Lord's plan for His house, we studied our text from First Kings 18. We found a key in Elijah's ministry when he "repaired the altar of the Lord which had been torn down...[with] twelve stones according to the number of the tribes of the sons of Jacob, to whom the word of the Lord had come, saying, 'Israel shall be your name'" (1 Kings 18:30-31). "Primitive," "intimate," and "majestic" became operative words in our discussions.

After many meetings and much prayer, Philip completed a design that satisfied all of us. The new building would be in the shape of a Greek theatre with a round central platform surrounded by twelve large, rough Mount Carmel stones. The congregation would be seated closely around the raised altar. From an overhead skylight, a shaft of light would break into the auditorium and illuminate the central platform. Ten cantilevered columns would support the high ceiling, affording an unobstructed view of the platform for each of the four hundred seats designated for the first phase.

The walls of the sanctuary were designed with a series of large arched windows in order to reflect the existing architecture of Stella Carmel and the Middle East. These walls would open out to provide seating for an additional 450 people. Surrounding the sanctuary outside would be a large semi-circular verandah. From the roof, we would be able to see the Mediterranean Sea to the West and a magnificent panorama of Galilee to the East. This is the highest point on Mount Carmel and a wonderful place to pray. Classrooms and offices, as well as the large, mandatory bomb shelter, would be housed in the lower level beneath the sanctuary.

The vision we received from the Lord for the new building is that it would be a house of prayer, praise, and proclamation of the gospel to Israel, the Middle East, and the nations:

> "'For My house shall be called a house of prayer for all nations.' The Lord God, who gathers the outcasts of Israel, says, 'Yet I will gather to him others besides those who are gathered to him'" (Is. 56:7-8 NKJ).

Isaiah was the first prophet to give clear expression to the coming of the "one new man" of Jew and Gentile through the Messiah Yeshua. It was out of this vision of the "one new man" that Carmel Assembly and House of Victory, where Jews and Arabs live and worship together, were born. The Lord has called us to be a ministry of reconciliation, interceding for Jews and Arabs in Israel and the surrounding Muslim nations.

Even before our building was complete, the prayer vision began to be fulfilled. In November 1995, the first "prayer summit" was held at Stella Carmel. Thirty Jewish, Arab, and Gentile leaders from Galilee and the Carmel range sought the face of Yeshua together for three days. Since then, we have met periodically in different areas of Galilee, to bear one another's burdens and pray for revival. We held our second "summit" in November 1996. Intercessors and prayer groups from Europe, Britain, Australia, New Zealand, Canada, Zimbabwe, South Africa, Finland, and the United States of America have also heard the call to come to Mount Carmel and to intercede with us.

After the agreement for the land was signed and the design for the building was completed, the months dragged on. We realized we were in yet another prayer battle to obtain our building license. We sensed that corruption was involved, and we prayed for the Lord to put an honest person on the governmental authority in charge of making the decision to grant us our license.

In the meantime, a third pastor, Eitan Shishkoff, joined our leadership team. He had a burden to reach Russian-speaking immigrants. Near the end of 1995, we commissioned Eitan, his family, and about ten other families from our community to plant another new congregation in Haifa. They rented a warehouse in a Haifa suburb near the port, in an area for which we had been praying for five years. The new ministry is called Ohalei Rachamim, "Tents of Mercy."

In mid-December 1995, I returned to New York to play Isaiah in the annual holiday musical at Times Square Church. I also brought a message on "The Spirit of Elijah" and asked the congregation to pray that we would receive our building license on Mount Carmel. About two thousand people cried out to God. The next day while I was in the church office, Barbara Mackery brought me a fax. It read: "We just received our building license. Love, Karen." When I reported this dramatic answer to prayer at the weekly Times Square Church prayer meeting a few days later, a collective roar of thanks and praise went up from the congregation.

On January 27, 1996, I plunged a gold-painted shovel into the field on the top of Carmel. Karen led Jews, Arabs, and believers from abroad in praise and thanksgiving to the Lord.

We had made the decision to use volunteer labor in the construction of the building. As we broke ground that day, the first work party from the USA had just arrived. A few days later, men and women began to tie steel onto frameworks as deep foundations were chopped into bedrock. Soon the first truckloads of concrete were poured.

The Lord continued to provide the right people for His work. Teams of short-term volunteers stayed at the retreat center as they worked on the building. One American from Las Vegas said the Lord told him to come and work until the building was finished. He built a little wooden cabin among a grove of trees alongside the building site. We now had a night "watchman."

When a handful of long-term volunteers arrived, we rented a large apartment. It quickly filled up with workers from Switzerland, France, England, Finland, and other countries. Patmos International in Finland sent us a large shipment of much-needed wood and tools, as well as hundreds of Russian Bibles. We also received another sizable gift of wood from a believer in Sweden.

Nine months into the project, volunteers from twenty different nations and many different denominations had worked on the building. Times Square Church also regularly sent teams that then took back firsthand reports to New York of what the Lord was doing on Mount Carmel. The workers had daily devotions and prayer times, and the Lord did deep things in them as they labored together. As Jews and Arabs, delivered addicts and alcoholics worked alongside each other and prayed with the foreign volunteers, we witnessed God's vision for His house beginning to be fulfilled. A "one new man company" was building the Lord's house!

As the foundations of the building were laid, the Lord also started to do a deeper work in the members of our congregation. He began with the leaders and our wives. A prophetic word came forth that He was about to take us on a new path: "You have not passed this way before...Consecrate yourselves, for tomorrow the Lord will do wonders among you" (Josh. 3:4-5).

We called our home groups together, and held a meeting focused on repairing strained relationships and releasing old hurts that had been repressed for months and years. In some relationships, both inside and outside families, communication had broken down. People went to one another and asked for forgiveness. They affirmed their love for each other. The Lord began to heal His "living stones." I sensed I was seeing a literal fulfillment of Micah 7:14 (NKJ):

> "Shepherd Your people with Your staff, the flock
> of Your heritage, who dwell solitarily [alone]
> in a woodland, in the midst of Carmel."

As the Holy Spirit showed us how to put God's house in order, we installed Reuven Ross as our third leader. Reuven is a Jewish believer who, with his wife Yanit, had lived in Jerusalem for some years. The two of them also have had an international teaching ministry in a number of countries.

Two and a half years earlier, Reuven and Yanit conducted a leaders' conference in Monterrey, Mexico. One night, during a time of deep intercession for the Mexicans, a spirit of travail suddenly came on Reuven for Karen and me, although he hardly knew us. Months later, when I saw him at a prayer conference in Jerusalem he told me how he had been praying for me and asked if he could come up to Haifa to see Carmel Assembly and House of Victory.

In 1994, after much prayer, Reuven and Yanit moved to Haifa to labor with us. Yanit is a gifted biblical counselor. Both she and Reuven impart the Lord's vision for disciple-making with small groups of men and women in our congregation. They also have had a fruitful ministry among singles and have just published their first book on the subject, entitled *Flying Solo: A Higher View of the Single Life.* We believe they will head up a much-needed counseling center in the new building.

In order to spiritually strengthen the men and families of our congregation, I began to teach a monthly men's "Priesthood Series," asking the question, "Is There a Priest in Your House?" The impetus came from Joshua's charge to the children of Israel: "But as for me and my house, we will serve the Lord" (Josh. 24:15c). Joshua, a father and husband, was a man in right relationship to God, his wife, and children. I have found that many times men who should be the spiritual leader in their families simply are not. I believe that a major cause of weakness in the body of Christ is that husbands and fathers often shirk their God-given responsibility to serve as the priest in their own households. Many families are wounded and open to attack because men have not exercised godly leadership in their homes. We continued to meet monthly, becoming more accountable to the Lord and each other.

The Lord has called us to engage in prayer warfare against the powers of darkness assigned to oppose the purposes of God on this mountain. "Carmel" means "God's fruitfulness" or "God's vineyard," but today, false religions and New Age cults flood the Carmel. Just down the mountain from the new worship center is an artists' village, populated by artists who practice various New Age, witchcraft, and Kabala (Jewish mysticism) techniques. Once, Karen and I were invited to live there because we were both artists and perceived to be "spiritual people." One sculptress told us that "the spirits" have been summoning these creative people from different parts of the world to live on Mount Carmel. It is clear to us that, "...our struggle is not against flesh and blood, but against the rulers, against the powers, against the world forces of this darkness, against the spiritual forces of wickedness in the heavenly places" (Eph. 6:12).

In addition to the spiritual weapons of prayer and fasting used to pull down strongholds (see 2 Cor. 10:4), a vital aspect of our warfare on Mount Carmel is praise and the proclamation of the Lord Yeshua, *"Adonai Tzevaot"*–the

Lord of Hosts. He has strategically placed us on this mountain to take an offensive stand, aggressively declaring His victory over the powers of darkness.

As the worship leader for the congregation, Karen has sought the Lord for vision and direction concerning our praise and worship. One key passage the Lord gave her was Isaiah 42:11-13:

> "Let them shout for joy from the tops of the
>   mountains.
> Let them give glory to the Lord...
> The Lord will go forth like a warrior,
> He will arouse His zeal like a man of war...
> He will prevail against His enemies."

The Lord is releasing new prophetic songs in Hebrew through members of the congregation in order to equip us to "shout to God with a voice of triumph" (Ps. 47:1 NKJ). We stand upon His Word that He is King of kings and Lord of lords. We believe that, as the Lord goes forth like a warrior and prevails against His enemies, the day will come when His glory will be seen and the fire will again fall on Mount Carmel. Our prayer, like Elijah's, is that the people may know that He is God in Israel and will say as they once did, "The Lord, He is God! The Lord, He is God." (See 1 Kings 18:37-39.)

Karen and her musical partner Joy Griffiths continue to write new songs in Hebrew and English, many of which have now been recorded on internationally released albums.

Much of the focus of our prayer, praise, and proclamation is toward this genuine revival we believe is coming to Galilee and Carmel, according to what we see promised in the scriptures. The first verses of Isaiah 9 refer specifically to "Galilee of the Gentiles":

> "The people who walked in darkness
> Have seen a great light;
> Those who dwelt in the land of the shadow of
>   death,
> Upon them a light has shined"
> (Is. 9:2 NKJ).

We know that Jesus fulfilled this verse when He lived and ministered in Galilee, because Matthew 4:14-16 says so. But I believe the next verses are being fulfilled now:

> "You have multiplied the nation
> And increased its joy;
> They rejoice before You
> According to the joy of harvest...
> As in the day of Midian" (Is. 9:3-4 NKJ).

In the last five years, God has "multiplied the nation." He has packed Galilee and Haifa with thousands of immigrants from the former Soviet Union and Ethiopia. When one stops to put gas in his car in Galilee today, a Russian-speaking rocket scientist or doctor may be manning the pump. The spiritual climate of the nation has changed radically. These immigrants have been oppressed, spiritually starved people who are open and hungry for truth. "The day of Midian" refers to the Galilean revival of Gideon's three hundred. When the members of Gideon's little band "each stood in his place around the camp," and blew their shofars, all the enemy ran away (Judg. 7:21-22).

Not only is revival promised for Galilee, but also for Mount Carmel:

> "Until the Spirit is poured upon us from on
> high,
> And the wilderness becomes a fruitful field,
> And the fruitful field is counted as a forest"
> (Is. 32:15 NKJ).

"Fruitful field" is a translation of the Hebrew word *carmel*, meaning "God's fruitfulness." This verse is carved in Hebrew over the largest synagogue in Central Carmel, near where we live. The rabbis know revival is coming; they just don't know yet that it is coming through Yeshua. We long for the fire to fall again and to see another Mount Carmel miracle.

The Lord told Ezekiel to "prophesy to the mountains of Israel" to "hear the word of the Lord...for My people Israel; for they will soon come...and I will multiply men on you, all the house of Israel" (see Ezek. 36:1-10). What a privilege and responsibility we have to serve the Lord on one of the mountains of Israel in the days the prophets foretold millennia ago. God says He is going to vindicate the holiness of His great name when: "I...will bring you into your own land. Then I will sprinkle clean water on you, and you will be clean; I will cleanse you from all your filthiness and from all your idols. Moreover, I will give you a new heart and put a new spirit within you... and cause you to walk in my statutes.... Then the nations that are left round about you will know that I, the Lord, have rebuilt the ruined places...I, the Lord, have spoken and will do it" (Ezek. 36:24-27,36).

He told His prophet to prophesy to a valley full of dry bones. Ezekiel obeyed, and "they came to life, and stood on their feet, an exceedingly great army. Then He said to me, 'Son of man, these bones are the whole house of Israel'" (Ezek. 37:10-11a). Revival is coming to Israel. God said it. He will do it.

When Karen and I were married, I did not fully appreciate the significance of her being a Jew and me a Gentile. As we were called to Israel, the Holy Spirit began to birth in us the vision of a "one new man company":

> "For He Himself is our peace, who made both groups into one, and broke down the barrier of the dividing wall, by abolishing in His flesh the enmity, which is the Law of commandments contained in ordinances, that in Himself He might make [create] the two [Jew and Gentile] into one new man, thus establishing peace, and might reconcile them both in one body to God through the cross" (Eph. 2:14-16).

The word for "one" in Hebrew, *echad*, stresses unity, while recognizing diversity within that oneness. For instance, Adam and Eve were to become "one" flesh (Gen. 2:24). In another example the people gathered with "one [*echad*] voice" (Ex. 24:3). The most well-known use of *echad* is in the *Sh'ma*, the central confession of the Jewish faith: "Hear, O Israel! The Lord is our God, the Lord is one!" (Deut. 6:4). The vision of the "one new man company" we seek to embody is not a unity of conformity, but a unity in diversity made up of Jews and Gentiles.

The Greek word for "new" in Ephesians 2 is *kainos*. It means "fresh, novel, unused, unique"–not new in time, but new in form and quality. This "new" is of another nature in contrast to what is "old." It is of a different essence and spirit. The apostle Paul wrote that we are "a new [*kainos*] creature" (2 Cor. 5:17), a people with a new foundation and formation. This creation is manifested as Jew and Gentile take on the very nature and life of the Son of God: "...put on the new [*kainos*] self, which in the likeness of God has been created in righteousness and holiness of the truth" (Eph. 4:24).

Jesus reconciled us in one body through the cross. The cross is the only place where this new identity may be obtained. We have access together to enter the holy place by the blood of Yeshua, by a *new* ("freshly slain") and *living* way, which He inaugurated at the cross (see Heb. 10:20).

This "one new man" has always been in the heart of God. "[He] has saved us, and called us with a holy calling, not according to our works, but according to His own purpose and grace which was granted us in Christ Jesus from all eternity" (2 Tim. 1:9).

There are well-intentioned Jewish brethren in Israel who believe the Lord wants to "restore" His people by bringing them back to re-embrace the Mosaic Law. They believe that "restoration" means to bring back the former conditions. However, when God restores someone or something, the biblical principle is that the person or situation is always increased, multiplied, and made new so that the latter state is significantly, radically, supernaturally better than it was previously. The two disciples on the road to Emmaus did not recognize the resurrected Jesus because they were "soul-bound," which caused their near-sightedness. God never goes backward; only people do.

Paul's letter to the Ephesians (written to both Jew and Gentile) unveils the "mystery" of God's eternal purpose for His body on earth as no other portion of sacred Scripture does. God's secret intention, the deepest longing of His heart, is revealed: Jew and Gentile recreated as one in Messiah, in order to form "one body and one Spirit...with one Lord, one faith, one baptism, in one God and Father of all" (Eph. 4:4-6). This revelation was so radical that the apostle Paul had to introduce a new terminology in order to describe this new peoplehood of God–the "one new man."

We are the stones of a spiritual community seeking to define and express a oneness (unity in diversity) where Jews can be Jews–Arabs can be Arabs–and Gentiles can be Gentiles. However, we are called to be "ONE" and "NEW," in essence, quality, and form–a "NEW CREATION," which has been planted on Mount Carmel by the Spirit of God. We are going a way we have never gone before–and we have just begun.

Epilogue

Recently, I met with the leadership team at House of Victory to talk to them about preaching. I explained that it is a holy calling to become "oracles of God" and to only speak what we truly receive from Him. As I drove out of the compound, I paused and looked at the old white building and the beautiful grounds bursting with spring flowers. Six years earlier, the Gulf War had just ended and the work had begun. I thanked God for our "one new man" staff: Eric, a Gentile married to an Arab; Danny, a Jew married to a Gentile; and Joseph, an Arab whose wife is from Lebanon. The house was in order.

I drove down to the Mediterranean and took the coastal road along the northwestern tip of Mount Carmel. After a few miles, I turned to go up the mountain road to the top where I had a meeting with our building team. I thought about the four days of prayer preceding Passover, which had just concluded. More than one hundred intercessors from Europe, America, Singapore, and Australia had wept with us for "the lost sheep of the house of Israel." We prayed fervently for the Passover Lamb to reveal Himself. There were more than two hundred people at our Passover Seder. Perhaps a dozen Jews heard the gospel for the first time. A Jewish drug addict, who had been in jail the previous day, asked me to pray with him to receive Yeshua, his Messiah.

The road from the sea up the western side of Mount Carmel is old and narrow. There is a bridge where only one car can pass at a time. The road is lonely and few cars use it. The terrain is a rocky and primitive nature reserve. Olive trees abound. The road to Mount Carmel is the path to God's fruitfulness, the way into His vineyard. It is an upward climb for those who long for God's highest in their life. These are the ones who, with the apostle Paul, can truly say,

"Forgetting what lies behind and reaching forward to what lies ahead, I press on toward the goal for the prize of the upward call of God in Christ Jesus" (Phil. 3:13b-14).

Shalom from Mount Carmel
Passover, 1997

Afterword

(Third Printing)

On Shabbat, September 12, 1998, we dedicated the new worship center on the top of Mount Carmel. Approximately one thousand people from Israel and the nations joined us that day for the two historic meetings. We have been told that this is the first indigenous Israeli congregation to build a meeting place in Israel in perhaps two thousand years. Since breaking ground in January 1996, over five hundred volunteers from forty-nine nations have offered their time and skills in the construction of the building.

The main sanctuary and surrounding colonnade were packed to standing room only. Karen and our worship team took their places on the raised platform surrounded by twelve large stones, which were hewn from the bedrock upon which the foundation stands. Above them, light streamed down through the skylight upon our sacrifice of praise, as we proclaimed, "O Lord, You are holy, enthroned on the praises of Israel" (see Ps. 22:3). We continued praising God in Hebrew, Arabic, and English, singing several of the new songs the Lord had given us for the occasion. As the worship time came to a climax, we sang a song based on Elijah's prayer, which he cried out from this same mountaintop:

> "Answer me, Lord, that the people may know
> That O Lord, You are God
> And You're turning them and calling them...
> The Lord is God! The Lord is God!
> The Great I AM, the Holy One!
> The Holy One of Israel, the Lord of life!
>   The Lord is God!
> A voice of one crying in the desert
> Prepare the way of the Lord
> And the glory of the Lord shall be revealed
> And all mankind shall see it..."[1]

David Wilkerson and his wife Gwen had flown in from New York City for the celebration. In his morning message, Pastor David challenged us to long for the glory of God to return to Israel. That glory will be the true nature of Christ manifested in and through His purified body. At the conclusion of the morning service, leaders from the land (Jews, Arabs, Gentiles) came forward. We held hands and prayed, dedicating ourselves afresh to God, as we are the ones "being built together for a dwelling place of God in the Spirit" (Eph. 2:22 NKJ).

When the evening meeting began, it had not rained in Israel for over four months. Just as David Wilkerson prophesied a coming stock market collapse in America, there was a tremendous crash of thunder and flashes of

---

1. First Kings 18:37-39; Isaiah 40:3,5 © 1997, J. Griffiths.

lightning. Then we heard the rain begin to pour onto the skylight above him.

At the conclusion of the service, we presented Gwen Wilkerson with a silver and gold necklace created by an Israeli believer. Gwen poured out her heart to the congregation as she shared of the faithfulness of God. She gave personal testimony of how God had healed her and sustained her through every trial. Engraved on the necklace in Hebrew were the words, "Heal me, O Lord, and I will be healed" (Jer. 17:14a).

As I looked around at the beauty of the building and of the faces of all those gathered together to worship, I saw before me a demonstration of the power and love of God. It was yet one more reminder of His faithfulness as we continue to walk with Him on His road to Carmel.

Additional Ministry Materials Available from David & Karen Davis

BOOKS:

David Davis

The Elijah Legacy
> (The Life and Times of Elijah – The
> Prophetic Significance for Israel, Islam and
> the Church in the Last Days)

The Rise and Fall of Islam
> (Booklet)

AUDIO MESSAGE SERIES:

David Davis

"The Spirit and Power of Elijah"
"Restoration of the Prophetic"
"Fire on the Mountain"
"The Anointing"
"The Glory of the New Covenant"
"Islam, Israel, and the Church"

MUSIC CDs:

Karen Davis

"Yeshua" (*formerly titled "Behold His Glory"*)
"Sar Shalom"
"Israel My Beloved"

...*continued*

...continued

VIDEOS

"Kehilat HaCarmel (Carmel Assembly)" DVD
*(presents an overview of the various
ministries of Carmel Assembly)*

"Fire on Mt. Carmel"
*(Powerful testimonies of reconciliation
between Arabs and Jews)*

"House of Victory"
*(Story of Israel's first Bible-based
rehabilitation center)*

If you are interested in ordering any of the above materials or if you would like to receive monthly prayer updates or the bi-annual newsletter sent out from this ministry, please contact:

**Kehilat HaCarmel
P.O. Box 7004
Haifa 31070
ISRAEL**

E-mail: info@carmel-assembly.org.il

Website: www.carmel-assembly.org.il